GOD'S UNFAILING PURPOSE
THE MESSAGE OF DANIEL

MICHAEL P. V. BARRETT

AMBASSADOR
EMERALD INTERNATIONAL

GREENVILLE, SOUTH CAROLINA • BELFAST, NORTHERN IRELAND
www.emeraldhouse.com

God's Unfailing Purpose

Cover design & page layout by A & E Media — Paula Shepherd

ISBN 1 932307 04 4

Published by the Ambassador Group

Ambassador Emerald International
427 Wade Hampton Blvd.
Greenville, SC 29609
USA
www. emeraldhouse.com

and

Ambassador Publications Ltd.
Providence House
Ardenlee Street
Belfast BT6 8QJ
Northern Ireland
www. ambassador-productions.com

TO ALAN AND JOAN CAIRNS

MY MINISTER AND HIS WIFE

FRIENDS, CO-LABORERS, AND EXAMPLES

TABLE OF CONTENTS

PREFACE

Where is God? That is often the question of skeptics, scoffers, and even troubled souls. Confessedly, the affairs of life seem frequently to justify the question. Trials and tribulations of one sort or another crowd our personal lives, while corruption, conflict, and catastrophe command the world scene. Indeed, where is God in all of this? Asking the question is fair enough; answering it demands caution.

Many simply factor God out of the picture altogether: Man is the master of his own fate and must struggle against all the barriers that life stacks against him. Life is every man for himself, and getting through the experience of the moment is the great goal. How the world relates to self is the chief concern. Others, professedly careful to keep God in the picture, define God in such a way as to make Him nothing more than a distant spectator who is interested in the affairs of the world but whose involvement is at best only reactionary to what He sees man do. Not only does God have no control over what happens, He has no knowledge of what happens until after the fact–just like the rest of us. Currently, this perverted and blasphemous concept of God is being touted in terms of Open Theism. This so-called theology argues that since God created man with a free will, even He must await the choices of the billions of free wills that at any moment combine and interact to create the next reality before He knows what to do next. So all the bad things that happen in life surprise God as much as us. He may really care about us, but there's not much He can do to help us in the times of trouble. Open

Theism promotes man to the throne and demotes God to the sidelines. Still others, rightly fearful to dethrone God, chafe under what they perceive to be divine insensitivity, blaming God for all their problems. Then there are those who take whatever the Lord gives with fatalistic stoicism rather than faith. To sum it up simply, there are many wrong answers to the question of where God is in all the issues of time and circumstance.

The old spiritual is far more accurate than the notions and denials of many theologians and expresses simply the essence of the truth I want us to see: "He's Got the Whole World in His Hands." Truth is unaffected by either ignorance or denial. The biblical answer is unequivocally to the point: "But our God is in the heavens: he hath done whatsoever he hath pleased" (Psalm 115:3). In another place, the Psalmist confessed, "For I know that the Lord is great" and that "Whatsoever the Lord pleased, that did he in heaven, and in earth, in the seas, and all deep places" (Psalm 135:5-6). In other words, there is no place outside the sphere of God's interest and involvement. This is good because not only is God great, He is also good and only does good things (Psalm 119:68). Since, therefore, God's goodness is just as infinite, eternal, and immutable as His greatness, His governing all things everywhere to accomplish His pleasure is a happy prospect. What could possibly be better than for the Creator and Sustainer of the entire universe to accomplish His good and perfect will–particulary when we know Him as well as our Savior? We may not always understand what God is doing with us at any given moment to accomplish His good will, but the more we rest in the reality of His goodness and greatness, the more we will accept it peacefully and joyfully as that which is best for us.

The absolute and supreme Sovereignty of God is perhaps the most comforting theological truth that God has graciously revealed to us about Himself–at least with reference to living out our time in this world. It is strange to me that this truth that reveals so much for the believer's comfort and assurance has been so commonly degraded to theological controversy, thus robbing so many Christians of its practical application. It is not my objective in this book to enter into theological controversy, but I do want to make much of the practical application of this profound truth for daily life. I want to do this by looking at time from a biblical perspective. This is important because time is where daily life takes place. Understanding time–whether past time, future time, or our time–requires trusting that absolute and supreme Sovereignty of God. The bottom line brings us back to the spiritual: He's got you and me, brothers and sisters, in His hands right along with the whole world. God's providence is unfailing.

The theme of this study involves deep theology and addresses significant details of both history and prophecy, but the book is designed with the lay person in view. I suppose it does not qualify for light reading, but I have avoided footnotes and technical interaction with other literature that may distract from the spiritual lessons that I trust are never far from the surface. Although this is not a scholarly treatment, the subject requires that I refer to what may be unfamiliar names and places as well as to the dreaded dates that tend to make history boring for some. Don't let the facts bog you down or distract you from the big picture. They are all pieces of the puzzle that fit together revealing the precision of God's unfailing purpose. Learning that the minute details of time are in His hands is a key part of the message even if you don't remember all the details.

I must express thanks to several people who have helped in the preparation of this work. I first of all give thanks to my employers, Geneva Reformed Seminary and Faith Free Presbyterian Church, for allowing me to work on the manuscript on company time. It was nice being able to reserve rising at 4:00 a.m. for deer season. I owe special thanks to Mrs. Cathy Simmons of the office staff at Faith Free Presbyterian Church for creating the charts and maps and to Mrs. Linda Abrams of the History faculty at Bob Jones University for checking the historical facts and theories. Their help and input were invaluable. Dr. Caren Silvester of the English faculty at Bob Jones University deserves my thanks (and yours) for her tedious labors in editing my grammar and style. Her work is always precise and insightful. I certainly must thank my wife, Sandra, for all of her help and encouragement. She read the first draft of each chapter, checked the final format and always said, "That's good Michael." Whether it is or not is beside the point. It was a happy day when, in the good providence of God, our times intersected and then converged. Of course, I thank Ambassador for its support and willingness to publish this work.

MICHAEL P. V. BARRETT
PRESIDENT OF GENEVA REFORMED SEMINARY
ASSOCIATE MINISTER OF FAITH FREE PRESBYTERIAN CHURCH
GREENVILLE, SC

INTRODUCTION

How goes the world? How goes life? Reflecting on these questions tends to evoke discouragement since time seems to advance only from crisis to crisis. Whether the problem occurs in our personal lives, our family, our neighborhood, our nation, or our planet, each exigency seems to precipitate the next. In this cycle of crisis, everything appears to be upside down. Evil is considered good; good is considered evil. Truth has fallen and is trampled in the streets by academic processions, political machinery, and populous parades. It seems that Christianity has become an ever-shrinking minority with lessening influence and dwindling numbers. Who is in control? If God is great and good, how can these things be?

Unfortunately, unbiblical answers to these questions invade Christian thought and further sink the soul into despair. Some Christians thrive on conspiracy theories. To them, every world, domestic, or financial crisis is orchestrated by some secretive few who rule absolutely—although surreptitiously—from some secluded conference room. Others console themselves with a last-day theology that generates a fatalistic passivism which contradicts biblical faith. They have a pie-in-the-sky optimism that in the end all will be well as God regains His lost control of this world that is now under Satanic government. The rampant evil of the present day happily heralds the soon end of time. Some professedly Christian thinkers and theologians have even postulated an "open theism" that claims bad things happen because God cannot prevent them from happening. God's good intentions are eclipsed by His basic inability to effect His will. God is good enough, but not great enough. These attempts to resolve the tension between God's goodness and greatness range from a happy worry to blasphemy.

I confess that I do not know why things are the way they are, and I often wish that things would more obviously, at least to my sight, work together for that good God has promised. Stumbling by sight has always been easier than walking by faith. But notwithstanding what I think I see, I have to believe that the Bible is true and that there is a throne that, while secluded from natural sight, governs absolutely with an unthwartable agenda. That throne is God's, and that agenda is His perfect will. Two things are certain: the kingdoms of this world will fail, and the kingdom of God will prevail.

No Christian denies the ultimate triumph of divine rule, but in the meantime we are confronted with circumstances that seem to belie divine control. Spiritual myopia distorts the perception of time with its focus on the immediate. Because the isolated "now's" of life are so vivid to sight, faith often fails to see what really is. Faith knows that appearance and reality are not the same, but what appears to be is, nonetheless, what we see. Faith must resolve the constant tension between experience and truth. The more it rests in the truth, the less the tension. This exercise of faith is not a wishful or positive thinking that crosses the fingers and squints the eyes, making believe that all is well. Faith's value is always defined in terms of its object. In His goodness, God has provided sufficient evidence both by His works and in His Word to keep us legitimately encouraged regardless of the circumstances of time. Having a biblically based theology of time is good for life.

A biblically sound theology of time flows directly from a proper view of the Lord Himself. How we view the Lord determines how we view life. How we view life mirrors how we view the Lord. Here is the simple fact of the matter: God is in absolute control of all things–the big issues of the world as well as the seemingly bigger issues of our lives. This is true whether man knows it or not, believes it or not, or likes it or not. Believing cannot make something true, nor can not believing make it untrue. The inviolable truth is that God is the sovereign King whose kingdom is universal; nothing is outside His domain. He does not try to control a democracy; He rules an absolute monarchy. Recognizing His rule and submitting to Him form the bedrock for a scriptural and practical time theology.

A theology of time centers on the divine work of providence. Providence is the temporal operation of the eternal God, through which He accomplishes His unfailing purpose. Providence is the constant and ordinary work of God whereby He preserves and governs His creation to the designed end of His glory. Included in that glory is the ultimate good of God's people. Every passing and progressing moment from the beginning of creation until the end of this age is planned and implemented by the all-wise, all-powerful, and all-good God. Don't confuse this wonderful truth with some pagan concept of fatalism that produces a "whatever-will-be-will-be" resignation. Belief in the sovereignty of God is the very opposite of fatalism; it never excuses passivity but rather motivates a confident activity. The affairs of life do not happen by blind chance; they happen as the all-wise God, who both knows and determines the end from the beginning, orchestrates them in perfect harmony. Not only are the affairs of life in God's hand, but His purposes are secure and unfrustratable.

The Preacher in Ecclesiastes affirmed: "I know that whatsoever God doeth, it shall be forever: nothing can be put to it, nor any thing taken from it: and God doeth it, that men should fear before Him" (3:14). Living in the constant awareness of God (i.e., fearing Him) puts a spiritual slant on things that is essential to a biblical philosophy of life, or, in other words, a theology of time. Providence assures us that there is a reason for everything, even though that reason may be hidden from our understanding. Faith lays hold of the great and good God and dispels the despair that so frequently grips us when we consider time and life apart from Him.

The Book of Daniel, a wonderful illustration of time theology, will provide the data for the study before us. Daniel knew precisely through the wisdom given him by God exactly how and where the world was going and what that meant for life's application. However, the Bible's most concise synopsis of a theology of time is the Book of Ecclesiastes. The message of this often maligned, misunderstood, and ignored part of Scripture constantly points to the eternal God who alone can satisfy man and who requires that the "stuff" of time be evaluated and used in light of the certain reality of eternity. Ecclesiastes 3:1-8, 11 is the key passage that defines the theology. "To every thing there is a season, and a time to every purpose under the heaven" (3:1). Following that all-inclusive statement, the Preacher employs literary genius to substantiate the conclusion in verse 11 that God has made everything beautiful or appropriate in His time. A series of fourteen pairs of twenty-eight specifically purposed times gives the overall impression that in the will of God there is indeed "a time to every purpose under the heaven." All the occasions of life are part of the divine order. The twenty-eight specific times mentioned form a sort of brachylogy (a condensed expression to designate the totality of an idea) and include, therefore, all kinds of time. The fourteen pairs are expressed as merismus (the linking of opposite terms to designate totality). For example, a time to be born and a time to die identify not only the unchangeably fixed moments of birth and death, but encompass all the moments in between. By the time we finish reading all the times for this and all the times for that, we've gotten the intended impression that there is indeed a time for everything. That's the point, and that's what I mean by literary genius. The inspired Preacher makes it clear that God determines our times and circumstances all for our good. It is comforting to know that "the righteous, and the wise, and their works, are in the hand of God" (Ecclesiastes 9:1). So a practical belief in the sovereignty of God will enable us to live through all the vicissitudes of life with confidence and good sense. Good sense always accompanies good theology. Theology is not mere theory.

If Ecclesiastes defines time theology and the proper thinking and behavior that accompany it, Daniel proves and illustrates how a God-centered and God-controlled theology of time works. Daniel knew that God was sovereign and that the course of time was in His hands. In language similar to that of Ecclesiastes, Daniel affirmed that it is the Lord who changes the times and the seasons (2:21). Daniel proved this truth with fantastic prophecies of God's plan that extended from the current events of his day to the certainty of both the first and the second advents of Christ. The details of these prophecies are significant and their precise fulfillment is precious, but sometimes so much attention is attached to the minutiæ of the predictions that their purpose is obscured or ignored. God never revealed the future to satisfy man's natural curiosity about it. Both the purpose and the nature of prophecy work to fuel faith. God reveals the future to affect the present. This is why prophecy is such an important element in establishing a theology of time, and Daniel used it masterfully.

I think prophecy's link to Daniel's theology of time will become clear when we remember the fourfold purpose of prophecy. First, prophecy *glorifies God by indicating that He is in control*. Because God rules, what will be is just as certain as what has been; His purpose will prevail. Prophecy is a dramatic way of displaying God's sovereignty, and thus it brings glory to Him. He knows the end from the beginning; therefore, He guarantees the end from the beginning. Nothing can frustrate or alter what He has determined.

Every so often the Lord revealed what was going to happen as proof of His dominion. As the Lord of time, He could do that. Isaiah 41 superlatively illustrates this truth. The Lord challenged idol worshippers to bring their "gods" to court to produce evidence of their worth as gods. The key challenge was the ability to predict the future: "Shew the things that are to come hereafter, that we may know that ye are gods" (Isaiah 41:23). When they remained silent, the Lord issued the verdict, "Ye are nothing" (Isaiah 41:24). The true God can do what idols cannot. The Lord gave evidence of His deity by telling how He would raise up one from the north (Isaiah 41:25). Later He identified that northerner as Cyrus, who would perform all of God's pleasure (Isaiah 44:28). He could identify Cyrus by name almost two hundred years beforehand because He was God. The relevance of this for a theology of time is significant. If God determines the future, it follows that He determines and controls the present as well. If nothing can frustrate His future purpose, nothing can frustrate His present purpose, either. Interestingly, what was Isaiah's future was part of

Daniel's present. I know that Daniel read the book of Jeremiah (see Daniel 9:2); I am fairly certain that he had read Isaiah as well. At least in Daniel's day, everything was under control.

Second, prophecy *encourages believers by inspiring confidence.* This confidence is the inevitable corollary to the assurance that God controls time and that regardless of appearances, the present is part of the execution of God's program. Looking in faith to the divinely revealed future should inspire confidence for service and duty by assuring the believer that his "now" fits precisely on the way to "then." A proper application of prophecy produces an active, bold, fervent, and confident performance of duty. The fiery furnace and lion's den testify to a viable theology of time.

Third, prophecy *intensifies the desire for God's will by increasing expectant hope.* Knowing what God has promised heightens the desire to experience and possess the promise. The more we contemplate the promise, the more we want the promise to materialize. The more details about the promise we know, the more intense the desire becomes. Prophecy is a means whereby God keeps hope alive and increases trust in and dependence on Him. Through prophecy, God incites us to want Him and what He has promised more than anything else. Daniel read Jeremiah's prophecy and prayed earnestly and fervently for it to be fulfilled. I would not be surprised if Simeon and Anna were counting Daniel's seventy weeks as they waited for the consolation and redemption of Israel to eventuate (Luke 2:25-26; 38). A biblical theology of time leads to the prayer, "Thy kingdom come."

Fourth, prophecy *motivates sinners to repentance and saints to purity by encouraging holiness.* If the Old Testament prophets teach anything about the use of prophecy, it is that prophecy motivates

7

repentance and purity. Joel, for instance, after describing the great and terrible Day of the Lord (Joel 2:11), issued a classic call to repentance: "Therefore also now, saith the Lord, turn ye even to me with all your heart, and with fasting, and with weeping, and with mourning: and rend your heart, and not your garments, and turn unto the Lord your God: for he is gracious and merciful, slow to anger, and of great kindness, and repenteth him of the evil" (Joel 2:12-13). The apostle Peter, describing the same Day of the Lord, concluded, "Seeing then that all these things shall be dissolved, what manner of persons ought ye to be in all holy conversation and godliness" (2 Peter 3:11). Nebuchadnezzar's natural curiosity about the facts of the future provided the opportunity for Daniel to press on the earthly king the claims of the eternal King. Daniel's bringing the future to bear on the present was a good application of time theology.

So we come back to the opening questions: how goes the world and how goes life? A sane and biblical answer to these questions requires a sound theology of time. As we try to answer these questions for ourselves, it is appropriate to consult one who knew the answer. That's why I want to study Daniel's theology. Realizing that verse-by-verse commentaries do not usually make for sustained reading, I will try not to get bogged down with technicalities of interpretation. So although I do not intend to write a commentary on Daniel, I do want to make some comments based on the book, paying attention to the salient details of the narratives and prophecies to help establish the big picture. Much of what was future for Daniel is now past for us; some of his prophecies have become history. I will relate the facts of history to the prophecies to show how precisely accurate were the predictions and to reason from history that it logically and legitimately follows that the yet-to-be-fulfilled prophecies are just as certainly accurate. Daniel makes it unmistakably clear that God's kingdom is certain.

Knowing that is crucial to a proper perspective of the time in which we live. Knowing that will inspire us to pray as Christ taught: "Our Father which art in heaven...Thy kingdom come. Thy will be done in earth, as it is in heaven." The coming of God's kingdom and the earthly execution of God's heavenly purpose go hand-in-hand. Perhaps Daniel did not pray those exact words, but his theology reveals the inseparable link between the two petitions. If any message prominently emerges from Daniel, it is that God's kingdom is coming and that God's will is being done on earth. Those two truths united establish the foundation for a theology of time. Those two truths united by faith will enable us to occupy the little bit of time that God has given us with confidence that our times are in His hands and that our times, no less than Daniel's, are a vital part of God's kingdom operation. Everything is under control. ❧

CHAPTER ONE

DANIEL: JUST THE FACTS

The Bible did not fall to earth from heaven complete and leather-bound. The Old Testament alone was written over a period of about a thousand years by different men, all of whom were inspired by the Holy Spirit. But each one lived in his own time and place; each one reflected and addressed the specific issues of his day. The truths of the Bible are universally and timelessly relevant, but they were first given to a specific people at a specific time to meet specific needs. The ultimate objective of our study of the Bible is to understand those universal and timeless truths and to apply them to our specific times and needs. An important part of Bible study is to learn what we can about the author, his times, and his particular circumstances. This discipline of study, called Introduction, deals with such issues as authorship, date, historical background, purpose, and theme of writing. So here are just some facts about Daniel–the book and the man.

PLACEMENT IN SCRIPTURE

In our English Bible, Daniel is the fourth of the Major Prophets. The book follows Ezekiel and precedes Hosea, the first of the Minor

Prophets. The designations "Major" and "Minor" refer only to the length of the written prophecies and imply nothing about the status of the prophet or the import of the message. Given the length of Daniel and the preponderance of predictions that constitute the message, placing the book with the Major Prophets makes sense.

In the Hebrew Bible, however, Daniel occupies a different place, between Esther and Ezra. The Hebrew Bible has three principal divisions: the Law, the Prophets, and the Writings. Although Genesis comes first in the Hebrew Bible just as in the English order, Chronicles concludes the Hebrew Bible, and the other books are arranged differently, too. Authorship was the criterion for placement. Only the writings of Moses constituted the Law, which we usually refer to as the Pentateuch, the first five books. Next, only those who were prophets by call and profession were included in the Prophets' section. Even a book of history such as Kings was part of the Prophets, because traditionally Jeremiah was regarded as the author. The rest of the authors, who were just as inspired by God as Moses and the professional prophets, were placed in the final section of the Writings. So here we find the poetry of David, the wisdom books of Solomon, and the narratives of Ezra and Nehemiah. Daniel was put in this section because Daniel was a bureaucrat by trade and not a prophet, notwithstanding the many prophecies in the book. His attention to history, however, does place him logically with Ezra and Nehemiah. (The only exception to the authorship criterion for book placement was the *Megilloth*, or scrolls. These books, regardless of authorship, were part of the Writings. These five books–Ruth, Song of Solomon, Ecclesiastes, Lamentations, and Esther–were kept together because of their liturgical use at various holidays in the Jewish religious calendar.

Given the common format of the scroll rather than the codex [book form] that we are familiar with, it was just more convenient to keep these regularly used books in one place.)

It is important for various reasons to remember the Jewish criterion for placing Daniel in the Writings instead of the Prophets. The issue was authorship alone. Liberal scholars usually argue that Daniel was in the Writings because, according to their theory, the book was written too late to be included in the Prophets. Few books in the Old Testament are attacked as vehemently as Daniel. It is far beyond the scope of my purpose in this study to address and rebut all of the liberal attacks leveled against Daniel. Let me just note that the attack reflects an unbiblical view of the inspiration and canonicity of Scripture generally, as well as a denial of the possibility of supernatural prophecy. This denial extends specifically to a rejection of the historic character of Daniel as the author. I am aware that refuting the claims of critics is a vital element of Introduction, but for now I am concerned with the facts of Daniel and not the denial of the facts by unbelief. This brief criticism must suffice.

LANGUAGE

Daniel is one of four books in the Bible written in more than one language. Greek is the unique language of the New Testament, and Hebrew is the principal language of the Old. Four books in the Old Testament, however, use Aramaic as well as Hebrew: Genesis, Jeremiah, Daniel, and Ezra. Aramaic is an ancient and distinct Semitic language very much like Hebrew. With the exception of Laban's two Aramaic words recorded in Genesis 31:47, biblical Aramaic comes from a time when Aramaic was the lingua franca of the ancient Near East. This simply means that it was the language of international communication, much as English is today. For more than a thousand years, Akkadian, the ancient and native language of southern Mesopotamia, was the lingua franca, but beginning perhaps as early as the 8th century B.C. Aramaic, the ancient and native language of northern Mesopotamia, was replacing it in that capacity. Second Kings 18:26 hints at this shift. When Sennacherib, the Assyrian king, sent his representative to hurl threats against Jerusalem, the representatives of Hezekiah implored, "Speak, I pray thee, to thy servants in the Syrian language; for we understand it: and talk not with us in the Jew's language in the ears of the people that are on the wall." What the Authorized Version translates as "Syrian" is what we are calling Aramaic. Jeremiah, as well, indicates the international use of Aramaic when he instructs the soon-to-be exiles what they should say in Aramaic when confronted with the idolatry of their foreign captors: "Thus shall ye say unto them, The gods that have not made the heavens and the earth, even they shall perish from the earth, and from under these heavens" (10:11). The several letters between Palestine and Persia recorded in Ezra 4-7 are classic examples of how Aramaic was used in international communications.

Daniel was among the first of Jeremiah's anticipated exiles to Babylon, and I wonder how many times during his expatriation he quoted Jeremiah 10:11. But that is just a matter for wondering; the fact is that the Aramaic portion of his book, 2:4b–7:28, corresponds well to the international use of the language. Significantly, the subject matter of this portion, starting with Nebuchadnezzar's dream of world history and ending with Daniel's vision of the same, has universal implications and applications whereas the Hebrew sections, although dealing in part with the same issues, carry a more specifically Jewish application. But whether using Hebrew or Aramaic, Daniel was supernaturally inspired by the Holy Spirit to write the Word of God.

DATE

Assigning dates to biblical books is a little complicated since our calendar reckoning differs from what was used in either Old Testament or New Testament times. But since our reckoning system is what we know and use, we customarily insert our own dates into the ancient time line. Plugging in our dates does not always yield precise results, but neither should it be regarded as mere guesswork. Scholars use two kinds of evidence for establishing these dates: relative chronologies and absolute chronologies. Relative chronologies involve simply putting names and events in sequential order. Absolute chronologies require the insertion of an actual calendar date in the sequence. These actual dates are often calculated from some ancient documentation mentioning an astronomical event, such as an eclipse. Although I am clueless as to how to calculate and deduce when and where eclipses occurred and will occur again, others, happily, are not. So we rely on those calculations and conclusions. The fortunate thing is that we have plenty of evidence from the ancient world, both from the Old Testament and from the people of Old Testament times, to establish fairly accurate chronologies. I'm not going to go into all the evidence for assigning a date to Daniel, but I do want to emphasize that the date is not just being pulled arbitrarily from some hat.

Explicit statements in Daniel reveal his contemporaneity with the Jewish king Jehoiakim, the Babylonian kings Nebuchadnezzar and Belshazzar, and the Persian king Cyrus. On the basis of this sequential evidence, Daniel's life spanned the closing years of the 7th century well into the 6th century B.C. We don't know Daniel's exact age when he went to Babylon, but we know that he was taken captive in 605 B.C., not long after Nebuchadnezzar's famous victory at the battle of Carchemish. If he was a teenager when exiled, his birth would have been during the administration of Josiah, about the time Jeremiah started his ministry. We don't know exactly how long he lived, but we know that he was still alive when Cyrus defeated the Babylonians in 538 B.C. and that he continued to work for some time during the Persian administration under Darius the Mede. So most of Daniel's life and ministry took place in the 6th century B.C., and he most likely wrote the book toward the end of his career—let's say about 530 B.C.

Once again, my purpose is just to give the facts about Daniel without refuting the denial of the facts by liberal scholars. But I must mention the significant difference of opinion between theological conservatives and theological liberals about the date of Daniel. As a theological conservative I adamantly maintain that Daniel lived in the 6th century B.C. and that he personally wrote the book that bears his name. The common liberal view claims that an anonymous somebody wrote this book in the 2nd century B.C., probably about 168 B.C. The primary reason for positing this later date is the precision with which the Book of Daniel details events that took place during the period of the Greek Empire, particularly those concerning the Seleucid division of that empire. We'll get to those details in due course, but the point for now is that because liberal critics deny the possibility of supernatural prophecy, they must insist on classifying those details (especially in chapter 11) as history rather than prediction. Those of us who believe the Bible have no problem with explicitly flawless prophecies. Indeed, we expect them because we believe in the God who knows the end from the beginning. Ultimately, whether Daniel dates to the 6th century or the 2nd century is a matter of belief or unbelief.

HISTORICAL SETTING

Dating the book is one thing; understanding the significance of the date is another. Factoring in what we know about Hebrew history with the overall history of the ancient Near East marks the 6th century B.C. as a climacteric point on the timeline of world history. From the perspective of Hebrew history, Daniel's life bridged two distinctive periods: the pre-exilic period and the post-exilic period. That Daniel links the two means that he lived all the way through the exilic period. These periods resonate with theological principles and reveal that God keeps His word–whether words of promise or words of threat.

Comprehending the import of these three periods requires going back to the book of Deuteronomy. One of the great themes in Deuteronomy concerns God's promise of the land. God first promised the land as an integral element in the covenant He made with Abraham and his seed (Genesis 12:7; 15:18; 17:8). That promise was unilateral and unconditional. Although the promise concerned a real geographical territory whose borders can be found on a map, God infused the land promise with important spiritual and theological lessons. There was more to the land than dirt. Because I am a premillennialist, I still believe in the dirt factor, but that is beside the point for now–although it will be a point before we leave Daniel. Simplistically stated, throughout the Old Testament God used the land as an object lesson to represent the fullness of the spiritual blessing. Rest in the land was associated with the experience and enjoyment of God's presence. So notwithstanding the ultimately unconditional aspect of the promise, individual participation in the promise was conditioned by faith. Thus, according to Hebrews 3:19, the wilderness generation did not enter the land "because of unbelief" (see also the argument of Psalm 95: 8-11). This is where the theology of Deuteronomy applies. Not only did entrance into the land require faith; so did remaining in the land. Moses expressed clearly the terms of the land contract. First, if they kept the commandments and walked in the ways of the Lord, the Lord would bless them richly in the land (see 28:1-2, 8-13). Second, if they violated the commandments, particularly by going after other gods, the Lord would curse them (28:14-15), primarily by plucking them out of the land and scattering them among the nations (28:63-64). Third, if they returned to the Lord, the Lord would exercise compassion and graciously gather them from wherever they were scattered and bring them back to the land (30:2-3).

The checkered history of Israel mirrors each of these contractual points. Although their faith was not unwavering nor their obedience perfect, several high-water marks in Israel's spiritual development brought them victoriously into the land and enabled them to enjoy the promised prosperity and blessing. Sadly, it was not long before they tragically disobeyed and faithlessly pursued other gods. In keeping with His word, God expelled the people from the land, first the Northern Kingdom of Israel and then the Southern Kingdom of Judah. In one way or another all the prophets echoed Moses and warned the nation of the impending judgment. Jeremiah, particularly, picked up on the third point and countered his message of imminent exile with hope of restoration after seventy years. At least from the perspective of the Southern Kingdom, Daniel saw it all. Born in Judah and exiled to Babylon, he lived long enough to see Zerubbabel lead the first group of refugees back home.

While the Old Testament reveals the reasons for Daniel's situation, the political history of the ancient Near East details the method by which God accomplished His purpose. Even a cursory survey of that history boldfaces the Lord's absolute sovereignty over all the affairs of the world to accomplish His purpose. Although the then-current events had military and political explanations that would have engaged the news media of the day, they evidence over and again the truth of Proverbs 21:1—"The king's heart is in the hand of the Lord, as the rivers of water: he turneth it whithersoever he will."

Because God is totally sovereign, He can choose to work either with or without external means to accomplish His will. The Lord's behind-the-scene manipulation of nations was His primary method of executing the consequences stipulated in Israel's land contract. This means of accomplishing His will showed itself most obviously when the time came first for Israel and then for Judah to be expelled from the land because of their unbelief. The prophets Hosea and Amos, particularly, warned the Northern Kingdom that their rampant idolatry disqualified them from the land and that judgment loomed. Hearing the threat, however, did not cause them to pack their bags and leave their homes on their own. The Lord used the Assyrians as His instrument to effect the expulsion. Isaiah, with prophetic insight, identified the Assyrians as the rod of God's anger sent against the hypocritical nation (Isaiah 10:5-6). From a natural historic perspective, it is not surprising that the Assyrians were able to conquer Israel. By the 8th century B.C., Assyria, militarily and politically, had become the most powerful nation in the world of the Near East with their control extending throughout Mesopotamia all the way to Egypt. They ruled an empire. Secular accounts from the period detail a military genius and cruelty that stood unmatched. Certainly, neither Israel nor Judah possessed military machinery sufficient to resist Assyrian advance. But what is striking is the Assyrian policy of deportation used to control their conquered lands and people. It was an ingenious way both to demoralize a people and to reduce the threat of rebellion. An expatriated people would have little incentive to revolt in a land which was not their native soil. What is even more notable is the fact that in the history of warfare this seems to be the first time such a tactic was employed. In 722 B.C., Samaria, the capital of Israel, fell to the Assyrians. Deuteronomy's threatened exile had begun. In the providence of God at the very moment when His patience with idolatrous Israel had expired and the time of their expulsion had arrived, there was a mechanism in place to accomplish His word. Let me pose this question: Where did the Assyrian commanders get the idea of deportation? Remember Proverbs 21:1.

It is equally remarkable that Judah did not fall to the Assyrians. Because the sin of the south was not yet ripe for judgment, Judah was preserved. God's direct intervention in protecting and preserving Judah showed that He was the One in control. During the administration of Hezekiah, God, without using any human means, caused the mighty army of Sennacherib to retreat in confusion after slaying 185,000 soldiers in the darkness of a single night (Isaiah 37:36). But sadly, Judah's sin did ripen. Judah could not remain exempt from judgment.

Virtually every prophet in the Old Testament warned them that it was going to come. In the meantime the world went on, seemingly as normal. Not long before Judah's judgment, God dealt with the Assyrians. Nineveh, the capital city, fell to the combined armies of the Babylonians and Medes in 612 B.C. Politics and power skirmishes followed, and Babylon ended up on top. In 605 B.C., the Neo-Babylonian Empire begins with Nebuchadnezzar at the head. He continues the Assyrian policy of deportation, and Judah's exile ensues. It worked for the Assyrians; it would work as well for the Babylonians. The first wave occurred in 605 B.C. Daniel was a part of this wave. The second occurred in 597 B.C. King Jehoiachin, Ezekiel, and ten thousand others were part of this one. The third occurred in 586 B.C. This was the big one in which Jerusalem and the Temple were destroyed. On the surface what happened during this period was just the stuff of world events: Babylon was on a roll. Above the surface what happened was the direct operation of God's will on earth. God was on the throne.

One final observation remains. The third element in Deuteronomy's land contract concerned the return to the land. Jeremiah, who declared that the loss of land was God's will, also announced God's will to restore the land in seventy years. The execution of this return was just as much in God's hand and control as the exile. For seventy years the world went on. Babylonian king followed Babylonian king until finally, in the normal course of human events, one regime replaced another. In 539 or 538 B.C., a coalition between the Medes (the former allies of Babylon) and Persians under the command of Cyrus defeated the Babylonians. This is the same Cyrus that Isaiah had named a couple of hundred years earlier, identifying him as God's shepherd and God's anointed, who would perform all of God's pleasure by ordering the rebuilding of Jerusalem (Isaiah 44:28–45:1). At the beginning of his administration, Cyrus issued a decree that the peoples who had been exiled during the Assyrian and Babylonian empires, who were now scattered throughout his even larger kingdom, could return to their homelands. Cyrus even subsidized the rebuilding projects, a wise strategy to insure stability and peaceful loyalty throughout the vast Medo-Persian Empire. The exiles of Judah were included. At the precise moment when in the purpose of God it was time for Judah to return to the land, a mechanism was in place to effect that purpose. Let me pose this question: Where did Cyrus get the idea to let the exiles return? Remember Proverbs 21:1.

Although Cyrus and the Assyrian and Babylonian kings before him were ignorant of their manipulation by God and their role as the agents of divine providence, they were nonetheless subjects of God's kingdom. God certainly held them accountable for their transgressions against His law and dealt with them according to their works, but not even the worst of them could jeopardize God's agenda. The heart of every one of those kings was in God's hand, and He turned it in whatever way He desired to accomplish His will. In hindsight, it does not require much spiritual acumen to recognize God's amazing control over the nations of the Old Testament world. So let me pose this question: At what point in the history of world did God stop controlling the nations of this world?

In our hearts we know the biblically correct answer to this question. In our heart of hearts we know that God controls governments and the course of human events as much today as ever. Yet so often we live as though God at some point in history abdicated His throne in exchange for a bleacher seat. Too many Christians live as though God is pacing back and forth in heaven wondering what He will or can do if this or that political party gains power. At the very least, that is not a biblical view of God. Indeed, correcting this faithless notion is the issue of the entire study before us. But it is enough at this point to state that the times of Daniel make it clear that God governed then, and the message of Daniel makes it clear that God governs now and forever. Everything is still under control.

PURPOSE

Why Daniel wrote is inextricably linked to when he wrote. His divinely revealed and inspired message was relevant to the immediate needs of the day. Although the hindsight of history puts in clear focus for us the hand of God working in Daniel's time, Daniel and his fellow exiles obviously did not have the benefit of hindsight to interpret their circumstances. What the facts of history are for us were the facts of life for them. The potential for experience to cloud the facts was just as real for God's people in the 6th century B.C. as it is for us.

Even a couple of years before the problems started for Daniel, Habakkuk had difficulty understanding what was happening. The prospect of God's using the pagan Babylonians as the instrument of chastisement against the chosen nation was incomprehensible and seemed incongruous to the very nature of God. Remember Habakkuk's complaint to the Lord. "Thou art of purer eyes than to behold evil, and canst not look on iniquity: wherefore lookest thou upon them that deal treacherously, and holdest thy tongue when the wicked devoureth the man that is more righteous then he?" (Habakkuk 1:13). God's answer to Habakkuk was not to worry: "The just shall live by faith" (Habakkuk 2:4).

So regardless of what appeared otherwise, the Lord was in his holy temple (i.e., palace), and all the earth should, therefore, "keep silence before him" (Habakkuk 2:20). Regardless of what appeared at variance with divine governance, faith rested in the certainty that the earth would "be filled with the knowledge of the glory of the Lord, as the waters cover the sea" (Habakkuk 2:14). Habakkuk learned an important lesson of faith. The lesson of faith that he learned in chapter 2 resolved the problem for his faith in chapter 1 and led to the peace of faith in chapter 3. Perhaps we'll study Habakkuk another time.

Daniel's message confirmed for the Babylonian exiles the sensibility of that lesson of faith by proving with prophecy that all the earth, indeed, would be filled with the knowledge of the glory of God. Daniel detailed some of the specific divine steps leading to the unfailing purpose of providence: the glory of God. He wrote, then, to inspire and instill a confidence in God's people, who were under the jurisdiction of a pagan state, that God was in control and that everything was working flawlessly according to His purpose and plan. Their times were in God's hand. Faith in God's sovereignty is foundational for a proper perspective of time, a theology of time.

I don't think it is coincidental that Daniel's chief counterpart in the New Testament was written during similar circumstances to achieve a similar purpose. When John wrote Revelation, he was in exile, and the church was being oppressed by the pagan Roman state. The persecuted church in the 1st century A.D. was to learn from John's marvelous prophecies that God, for His own glory, ordained and controlled the most pagan, ruthless, and Christ-hating regime that would ever exist in the history of time. If God was going to manipulate and frustrate the coming Anti-Christ (I'm a futurist), then believers had no cause to worry about Domitian. The unchanging fact of God's sovereignty was the truth of comfort. It put their times in the proper perspective.

There has to be a point in this for us. I want Daniel's purpose in writing to the Jews of his day to be fulfilled for us today. If the future is fixed according to God's sovereign pleasure, then so is the present. That was the point for Daniel's present, for John's, and for ours. The present constantly changes, but only according to God's unchangeable purpose. I submit that there is hardly a more practical and comforting truth for God's people than His absolute sovereignty. It is tragic that theologians have so often reduced this truth to controversial debate or recondite theory, thus robbing believers of a comforting constant that makes getting out of bed in the morning and facing the day the sensible and sane thing to do. So as we move from the facts about Daniel to the theology of Daniel, I pray that the Holy Spirit will lead us into the truth and enable us to enjoy it. ⊰⊱

CHAPTER TWO

DANIEL: MORE FACTS ABOUT THE MAN

The times in which Daniel lived explain much about the book, and they also reveal much about the man. The credibility of a message often depends on the credibility of the messenger. That is a sobering thought for every minister of the gospel–indeed, for every Christian who owns the responsibility to declare the gospel message both by life and by word. The apostle Paul admonished Timothy, "Let no man despise thy youth; but be thou an example of the believers, in word, in conversation, in charity, in spirit, in faith, in purity" (1 Timothy 4:12). If Timothy needed a model of what Paul wanted him to do, all he had to do was consider the life of Daniel. Daniel is a wonderful example of the just living by faith. His life is a pattern of how to live daily in the light of theological truth. The autobiographical material in the book attests to Daniel's personal conviction that God is absolutely sovereign, that his times were in God's hand, and that there was thus no better time for him to live and to serve than precisely then. For Daniel, theology was not theory; it was the bedrock for life. He practiced what he preached.

We are more than 2,500 years removed from Daniel. Time tends to enhance our veneration of past saints, whether those mentioned in the Bible or in missionary biographies. Yet significantly, our justly high admiration for Daniel parallels that of his contemporaries. The prophet Ezekiel refers to Daniel three times on two separate occasions in his prophecy. Remember that Ezekiel himself was taken captive to Babylon in 597 B.C. By the time he arrived, Daniel had been there for about eight years. In that relatively short period, Daniel had earned a reputation for godliness and wisdom. For those in his own generation, he was "an example of the believers, in word, in conversation, in charity, in spirit, in faith, in purity." On one occasion, Ezekiel referred to Daniel's exemplary righteousness, putting him in the company of Noah and Job (14:14, 20). That was some testimony! On another occasion, he alludes to Daniel's wisdom (28:3). Daniel's God-given ability to discern between truth and error and the ability to implement his knowledge of truth properly in his own life marked him then and now as a paragon of pious virtue. The children's chorus "Dare to Be a Daniel" is good advice regardless of age.

Even before God revealed to Daniel the course of time to come, young Daniel evinced his grip on the theology of God's rule of time. Because so much of the book of Daniel proceeds from the facts about Daniel that we learn from the opening chapter, I want to outline a few thoughts about his life that validate his credibility as a witness to God's total sovereignty over the affairs of time. Since I do not intend to comment on every verse, it may help if you read Daniel 1 so that you have the details before you. I think three facts will stand out to you for attention: his predicament, his purity, and his prudence.

DANIEL'S PREDICAMENT

Our survey of the historical setting of Daniel highlighted both the politics and the theology that caused the Babylonian captivity. The first two verses of Daniel 1 do the same. Militarily and politically, Jerusalem did not stand a chance. Verse one states the observable fact that Nebuchadnezzar besieged Jerusalem. If there were newspapers in those days, Babylon's siege of Jerusalem would have been on the first page, maybe even the headline. Verse two, however, states a fact that is knowable only by faith: "And the Lord gave Jehoiakim into his hand." The force of this statement intensifies with the occurrence of the word "Lord." This is the word *Adonai*, the divine title that declares God the absolute owner and master of all. It is the title that especially designates His sovereign kingship. So although what King Nebuchadnezzar did on earth with all of his military might was expected and explainable, it was nothing but what the King of kings decreed from heaven. Heaven's throne ruled; God's will was done on earth.

From both the political and the theological perspective, Judah's plight made sense. Militarily, they were weak and could do nothing about it; religiously, they had sinned and therefore deserved it. But what about Daniel? Through circumstances beyond his control and through no fault of his own, Daniel became a captive in Babylon. At first glance, his captivity makes no sense. It seems as though he was indiscriminately caught in the dragnet of Providence. But God's special design for Daniel's good and ours required his relocation to Babylon. The circumstance that was chastisement for the nation as a whole was the occasion of testing, strengthening, and service for this young man. However, as it was happening, Daniel knew nothing about God's greater good. My guess is that it was an unhappy day for Daniel and his family when he was rounded up and hauled off against his will to a foreign land. It was a time for weeping: "By the rivers of Babylon, there we sat down, yea, we wept, when we remembered Zion" (Psalm 137:1).

Throughout his divinely prescribed predicament, Daniel experienced the preserving and protecting arm of Providence as well. The Babylonian officials recognized his natural abilities and so enrolled him in a three-year curriculum leading to sure employment in government work (1:4-5). The God who endowed Daniel with all of his natural talents in the first place also brought him "into favour and tender love" with the administration (1:9). From the beginning of his expatriation under the rule of Nebuchadnezzar to the end of his life, most likely under the rule of Cyrus (1:21), Daniel was under the absolute rule of God, a subject of the King of heaven.

This is why I think Daniel is such a credible witness to a viable theology of time. His belief and confidence in the sovereignty of his God affected his living. Throughout his entire ordeal, he never expressed even a hint of discontentment or bitterness about his lot in life. Rather than feel sorry for himself, he used every circumstance that God arranged as an opportunity to glorify God. I don't suppose Daniel knew this hymn, but I know he affirmed its sentiment:

> *My times are in Thy hand; My God, I wish them there;*
> *My life, my friends, my soul I leave entirely to Thy care.*
> *My times are in Thy hand; Whatever they may be,*
> *In joy or pain; 'tho dark or bright, as best may seem to Thee.*

DANIEL'S PURITY

There is an adage that goes something like this: A crisis doesn't make a man; it reveals a man. Daniel was not long in Babylon before he revealed his pious character. Because of his natural abilities, Daniel was enrolled in an elite school in which he received not only a top-notch education but also a stipend consisting of royal room and board (1:4-5). However, something about the daily provision caused Daniel to refuse to eat. With uncompromising resolve, he "purposed in his heart that he would not defile himself with the portion of the king's meat, nor with the wine which he drank" (1:8). The Hebrew word translated "defile himself" has religious implications. In simple terms, eating the daily provision from the king's table was against Daniel's religion. Recognizing something about the king's provision that countered his rule for faith and practice, he became a conscientious objector. Whether the food and drink had been part of some pagan offering that Daniel found offensive or whether it violated the levitical dietary laws that Daniel regarded as mandatory is a matter of speculation. What is certain is that despite the risk Daniel took his stand, fully confident that he would be better off with a bland diet that honored the Lord than with luxurious fare that violated his conscience. For a teenager to exchange a daily feast of exquisite offerings for at best a vegetable plate or at worst a bowl of mush was no insignificant trade. Later, the same God-consciousness that determined his diet in his youth kept him on his knees in his old age regardless of the threats against his life. The stakes became higher, but his beliefs consistently bound his practice.

Two things impress me about Daniel's stand for purity. First, he was not obnoxious about it. His request to his supervisor was principled yet polite. Too often those who take the proper position on biblical issues exhibit such an odious and ostentatious manner that their good is evil-spoken of, and any potential value in their testimony is squandered by their rudeness masked in pomposity and self-proclaimed piety. Daniel's example at the beginning of his career while in school and then again at the end of his career while facing the den of lions was consistent. Always willing to accept the consequences of his separatism, he never evidenced a cantankerous spirit as he remained uncompromising in his convictions.

Second, he remained pure in a place where sinning was easy. He was far from home. In that pagan culture, probably, no one would have thought twice if Daniel had eaten the food that was put before him. Everybody else was doing it; he would have been part of the crowd. However, Daniel's probity was determined not by his surroundings but by allegiance to his God. Ezekiel 8 records a startling contrast to Daniel's situation. By way of vision, the Lord showed the prophet what was really in the hearts of the people who were professedly worshipping the Lord in the Temple back in Jerusalem. Jerusalem had a long history as the place God had chosen for His name to dwell; it was the city of God of which glorious things were spoken (Psalm 87:3). Thus, Jerusalem should have been a place where sinning was hard. Yet in the Temple itself, Ezekiel saw a people who were committing almost inconceivable violations against the Lord. Purity, we see, is a matter of the heart, not the environment. The children's chorus again rings true:

> *Dare to be a Daniel,*
> *Dare to stand alone!*
> *Dare to have a purpose firm!*
> *Dare to make it known!*

DANIEL'S PRUDENCE

If anything about Daniel stands out more than his consistently pure testimony, it is his remarkable wisdom. The word "wisdom" in the Old Testament refers to the skill or ability to apply knowledge properly–whatever the sphere of that knowledge may be. Daniel, along with the rest of his classmates, possessed some degree of this wisdom naturally in various academic subjects. That's what qualified them for their special education and earned their scholarship (1:3). However, God chose to confer on them the gift of godly wisdom, which cannot exist apart from the knowledge and fear of God (see Proverbs 1:7; 9:10). That Daniel and his three colleagues feared God is evident from their pious behavior. That God gave them wisdom is the explicit statement of the text: "And for these four children, God gave them knowledge and skill in all learning and wisdom..." (1:17). As a result, the counsel that these four furnished the king was ten times better than that of any other of the king's advisors (1:20). In addition to this God-given knowledge and wisdom, "Daniel had understanding in all visions and dreams"(1:17). It was this special gift and ability that thrust Daniel to the front so often in the critical moments of his time. Furthermore, Daniel did not presume on his possession of these gifts: he was always careful to seek the Lord for new wisdom for each new need. For instance, Daniel did not venture to interpret Nebuchadnezzar's dream until first he sought the Lord (2:18). He was wise enough not to take credit for his gifts: "I thank thee, and praise thee, O thou God of my fathers, who hast given me wisdom and might, and hast made known unto me now what we desired of thee..." (2:23). That remains the prudent course: "If any of you lack wisdom, let him ask of God, that giveth to all men liberally, and upbraideth not; and it shall be given him" (James 1:5). Although Daniel had never read James, he knew how to get wisdom.

So if the credibility of the message does indeed depend on the credibility of the messenger, the message of Daniel deserves careful consideration. His character, his faithfulness, and his testimony remained steadfastly pure in dark and difficult days. Daniel was not an armchair prophet who speculated about spiritual issues and things to come. His theology was not theory; it was the foundation for his living. He illustrates well the kind of life that God blesses. Read Psalm 1 and see if you can trace the life of Daniel. It is not difficult at all to summarize Daniel's life in terms of that blessed man who separates from sinners, who delights in the Lord, and who prospers in whatever he does (Psalm 1:1-3). Daring to be a Daniel requires believing what Daniel believed. ❧

CHAPTER THREE

THE GLUE AND THE GOAL: INTERPRETING TIME

istory is more than simply a record of past people and
events. Likewise, prophecy is more than simply a pre-
record of future people and events. In my relatively
short life, I've experienced many things that have created all sorts of
memories–some good, some bad, some distorted, some revisionary.
But my life is hardly the stuff of history. If I were to record my
memoirs of ministry, family, or even hunting experiences, no one
but me would be interested. I have ministry, family, and hunting
aspirations for my future, but even if all the appointments and
plans in my Palm Pilot were to happen as scheduled, my day-timer
is hardly the stuff of prophecy. In the overall scheme of things, my
life is unimportant, and I have achieved nothing that will earn a
mention in a history of civilization textbook or even a survey outline
of church history. I did once make the list of *Outstanding Young Men
in America,* but that was a long time ago, and I have a suspicion that
my mother nominated me. At least I know she was one of the few in
the world who bought the book listing my name and credentials in

fine print along with thousands of others just as insignificant as mine. This is beginning to verge on depressing–perhaps the onset of mid-life crisis. However, I have read Ecclesiastes enough to know how time and memory work. The inspired Preacher observed, "One generation passeth away, and another generation cometh: but the earth abideth for ever" (Ecclesiastes 1:4). The monotony of the death-life cycle is fueled by the perpetual loss of memory. "There is no remembrance of former things; neither shall there be any remembrance of things that are to come with those that shall come after" (Ecclesiastes 1:11). Every tombstone testifies to a life that was full of incidents momentarily and personally important, but now forgotten. How many buildings and roads bear the names of individuals who for a brief while others thought to be important, but whose names are now nothing more than points for direction? Life goes on.

So if my life, as important as it is to me, does not merit historical or prophetical interest, what does? This question warrants some consideration as we begin our study of Daniel's theology of time. Daniel outlines time from his present to the two advents of Christ. From his vantage, most of what he recorded was future; from our vantage, much is now history with some future yet to come. There is, however, a long "in between" that passes without reference point in his outline. Of all that has happened according to his history and of all that will happen according to his prophecy, why does he record the particular points that he does and omit so many others that we might find interesting or helpful? Understanding a little about the nature of history and the nature of prophecy will help us in applying Daniel's theology of time to ourselves wherever we are in that long "in between."

THE NATURE OF HISTORY

The data base for history is everything past. But, as we have already lamented, not everything past constitutes especially significant history. Writing history requires not only knowledge of what has happened but also some criteria for selecting from that corpus of knowledge what is significant. Even if I were to write my memoirs, much in my past not even I would regard as important, and many things I would not want anyone else to know. For instance, my staring at a blank computer screen has eaten up a greater proportion of time during this writing session than actual composition, but my dullness of thought may not be what I want to admit in an autobiography.

The very nature of history hampers historians because of their limited knowledge of the past, and it also breeds just suspicion about every historical account because of the biased perspective of the recorder. In one way or another, every new generation of historians depends for knowledge in part on earlier records, which themselves suffer from the recorder's ignorance of all the facts and necessarily reflect some bias. The ancient chroniclers were usually employed by the royal court, and consequently they skewed their facts in favor of the throne. It was their job to justify or glorify official policies and ventures and to create a legacy for the king. Today, we call them "spin-doctors." Governments have always used them. Just because something is written in stone, it doesn't make it so.

I remember having to learn in school about various philosophies of history that governed each historian's perspective of the past and that also determined what he regarded as germane to proving that perspective. Hegel's dialectical determinism defined the course of history in the cycle of thesis, antithesis, and synthesis. Comte postulated a positivistic approach based on empirical facts that progressed according to evolutionary principles. Spengler's quasi-biological cycle with its process of birth, progress, and degeneration seemed to reverse the evolutionary notion with the premise that decay was inevitable. Toynbee's challenge and response theory implied that so long as a civilization could meet all of its external challenges, it could survive. I've just about exhausted what I remember from my school days, but what I remember is enough to reinforce the claim that every historian interprets what he knows in the light of some philosophical program. This explains why we can read accounts by different historians of the same historical "fact" and get completely different explanations of what "really" happened. For instance, we come away with antipodal views of America's Civil War depending on whether the historian connects with a northern or a southern bias. The same Lincoln is either one of America's greatest presidents or one of the greatest rascals that ever occupied the office. Whom are we to believe?

Here's the point as it relates to the Scripture generally and Daniel specifically. If writing a truly important and accurate history requires knowing everything about the past, as well as the ability to identify the salient parts from that body of knowledge, Scripture is the only truly significant history that exists. Only God is omniscient; only God is infinitely wise. Therefore, only God, the ultimate author of Scripture who knows everything, has the skill to select from what He knows to record a history that is both infallibly accurate and eminently significant. So at whatever point secular history disagrees with sacred history, we know that the secular historian was either mistaken about the facts or was misleading in how he presented the facts. We can be absolutely certain of two things as we read the Bible: it is true, and it is important. Nothing ever written is more true, and nothing ever written is more important.

I suppose I will never forget sitting in a History of Civilization class as a university freshman and hearing the larger-than-life voice of the professor defining history as "His story." That statement, although simplistic, is profoundly to the point–it says it all. From creation, this world with its aggregate of people and events has operated according to the guidance of divine providence. Every thing that has happened, is happening, and will happen happens on purpose. That purpose is the glory of God. Although all creation declares God's glory (Psalm 19: 1) and our salvation praises the glory of God's grace (Ephesians 1:6), nothing reveals the glory of God more than His Son, the Lord Jesus Christ. It is not surprising, then, that all of "His story" should find its focus in the person and work of Jesus Christ. The New Testament states that the incarnation of the eternal Son of God was in the "fullness of time" (Galatians 4:4). From the Lord's first promise of Christ in Genesis 3:15, every moment and every epoch progressed toward that fullness. Since Christ's ascension to glory, every moment and every epoch are progressing toward the final fullness of time when the Lord will come again. "His story" is, therefore, the history of redemption, and Jesus Christ is both the *clue* to history's meaning and the *glue* that holds it on course to its certain *goal*.

Daniel is a casebook example of "His story." On one level Daniel chronicles the expected–the rise and fall of political kingdoms. Yet above the obvious rule of earthly kings exists the overriding rule of the heavenly King. Daniel makes it clear that God gave kings their power to rule and controlled them absolutely. Nebuchadnezzar's dream of the colossus and Daniel's vision of the weird beasts revealed God's ordination of human governments and His ability to direct the course of human history. The Most High God was the Lord and King of heaven (4:37, 5:23) and, therefore, the Lord of kings (2:47). The big events of time were all part of God's plan. Significantly on an unexpected level, Daniel's history includes seemingly small events as well. The eating habits of four teenagers or the prayer life of one old man would normally not interest historians. But these were important to the Lord, and they reveal that providence operates on the personal as well as the world level. Nothing is too small to escape the Lord's concern, particularly nothing in the lives of His people. And Daniel certainly knew about the clue and the glue. From the pre-incarnate appearances of Christ in the fiery furnace and lion's den to the prophecies of Messiah's crucifixion and the coming of the Son of Man to receive the kingdom, Daniel brings everything to the touchstone of Christ.

Daniel is good history. Understanding the goal and glue of history should help us in understanding our own time. Our times are part of the ongoing history of redemption. We may not know how all the specifics fit into the big picture, but we know that they must and indeed do fit. Our times are an integral part of "His story."

THE NATURE OF PROPHECY

All of "His story" is going someplace, and prophecy is a divinely inspired means of giving us a certain preview of that divinely determined destination. Technically, not all prophecy is predictive, but for now I am referring to its predictive element. If Daniel is good history, it is also good prophecy. Many of Daniel's prophecies have already been fulfilled. Hindsight testifies to the absolute accuracy of his predictions and justifies the confidence that what is still future will take place just as precisely. Seeing how some of his predictions entered the annals of history establishes some important guidelines for interpreting those predictions whose fulfillment remains future. Since so much of Daniel is predictive, reviewing some aspects of prophecy is in order before we consider the details of his predictions that together with his history provide the biblical basis for our theology of time.

The nature of prophecy flows out of its fourfold purpose to glorify God, to encourage believers, to intensify desire for God's will, and to motivate sinners to repentance and saints to purity. Prophecy is designed to fuel faith, not to foster fatalism. While growing up, I heard often that prophecy is simply pre-written history, as clear as yesterday's newspaper. I appreciate the God-honoring sentiment which generated that statement, but the fact is that prophecy is not as clear as history. (Read the morning newspaper and then read Revelation with its multi-headed and multi-horned beasts and form your own conclusion.) I maintain that every divinely inspired prophecy will be actually fulfilled; in that sense it is pre-written history. But clearly hindsight is a better interpreter than foresight. We must acknowledge, therefore, some important principles as we incorporate Daniel's future into our time theology.

PROPHETIC AMBIGUITY

An intentional ambiguity inheres in prophecy. God reveals enough clarity to testify to His control of time and faithfulness to His word, but He does not make us privy to every single detail of His plan. For example, 2 Kings 7 illustrates this principle of prophecy plainly because it contains two specific prophecies of Elisha and their literal fulfillments: cheap food and the destiny of the doubter. Samaria was under Syrian siege and was suffering great famine. Elisha's prediction of abundant and cheap food seemed impossible and "a lord on whose hand the king leaned" let him know so. That doubt precipitated the prediction that the lord would see it but not eat it (2 Kings 7:1-2). Both of these were very specific predictions. The details of the fulfillment, however, make it clear that Elisha left out some key facts. Had he delineated how the lepers would find the camp of the Syrians abandoned with all the cache of supplies and how the doubter would be trampled by the hungry crowd rushing to buy some of the cheap food, the doubter would have been a fatalistic fool to accept the king's appointment to "have charge of the gate" (2 Kings 7:17). But enough was revealed to make it absolutely certain that the whole episode was "according to the word of the Lord" (2 Kings 7:16). The prophecy was clear, yet ambiguous. Prophecy reveals much about the future, but it doesn't reveal everything. Remember that in Revelation 10, when John heard the seven thunders, God instructed the apostle not to write what was revealed to him. That prohibition to write tells us that we do not and cannot know everything about the future. We are to believe what God has revealed and trust Him for the rest. He lets us see enough to assure us that all time, including our times, are in His hand and under His control.

PROPHETIC LANGUAGE

Let me suggest some specific things to keep in mind about the nature of prophetic language. First, prophecy tends to use symbolic language that must be interpreted figuratively. This is particularly true in the special category of prophetic style called *apocalyptic prophecy.*

Daniel is a casebook example of apocalyptic prophecy. For instance, Daniel's prediction of world empires in terms of strange, unnatural beasts cannot be interpreted literally without, quite frankly, being weird. Only science fiction would claim that a king of Greece was in reality a rough goat with a big horn between its eyes (Daniel 8:21). Let's not confuse a literal or actual fulfillment of prophecy with a pedantically literal interpretation of prophetic language. The bestial symbolism of Daniel refers to actual empires. Some connection between the strange beasts and the kingdoms they represent has been and will be actually fulfilled. Interpreting symbolism requires that we determine the point of relevance between the symbol and the actual referent without attempting to find a tit-for-tat parallel. The meaning of symbolic language does not reside on the surface; discerning the meaning requires careful thought. That's fine: pondering Scripture always proves beneficial.

Second, prophecy tends to use the language of imminency. This means that regardless of how distant the prophecy from its actual fulfillment, the prediction is made as though its fulfillment were impending, about to occur. This intentional temporal ambiguity is one of the most significant features of prophetic language. Since the time of fulfillment is not specified, the application of the prophecy is not limited. For prophecies to be precisely dated would effectively rob a given prophecy of its purpose to affect the present of all the pre-fulfillment generations.

Third, prophecy tends to link distinct epochal events into single predictive contexts, giving the appearance of a single event. This is called progressive prediction or prophetic telescoping. In a single utterance, the prophet makes multiple predictions, juxtaposing them without any indications of time intervals between them. The focus is on the certainty of the events, not the timing of them. It is this regular disregard for strict chronology that differentiates history from prophecy. Comparing what Daniel says about the resurrection with Revelation illustrates this disregard for time. Daniel telescoped two types of resurrection without specifying the time gap between them: one to everlasting life and another to everlasting contempt (12:2). Later, John revealed that a thousand years would separate these two resurrections (Revelation 20:4-5). Interpreters, depending on their views concerning the millennium, can do what they want with what that means, but the fact remains that Daniel linked together what John separated.

PROPHETIC FULFILLMENT

A failure to take into account these features of prophetic language has led to some confusion about the nature of prophetic fulfillment. Debate rages as to whether a given prophecy has a partial, single, or double fulfillment—or even multiple fulfillments. Part of the disagreement stems from imprecise definition of terms and part involves fundamental differences in hermeneutics. It is far beyond the scope of our study to deal with these issues in detail, so I will simply offer here my opinion. I suggest that a specific prophecy has a single fulfillment. That's easy enough to suggest but not always easy to defend. I do believe, however, that the single fulfillment axiom works well in almost every instance. If we remember the inherent "timeless" factor in prophecy, we should not be tempted to demand a near as well as a distant fulfillment just to rescue contemporary relevance for the prophet's audience. The temporal ambiguity guarantees its relevance; one fulfillment is all that is necessary.

There are a couple of types of prophecy, however, that lend themselves to the appearance of multiple fulfillments. First, some prophecies constitute a whole concept that comprises specific constituent elements. The fulfillment of the prophecy develops progressively from element to element until the completion of the whole. For instance, both Isaac and Christ constitute Abraham's promised Seed. Obviously, Christ was the main issue, but there had to be an Isaac before there could be the Christ. Isaac marked the beginning of the fulfillment of the messianic prophecy. I prefer phrasing it that way rather than that the promise was fulfilled in Isaac and then again in Christ. The prophecy that the Seed of the woman would bruise the serpent's head seems to have a progressive fulfillment as well. Hebrews 2:14 indicates that the death of Christ was the means of destroying "him that had the power of death, that is, the devil." That Paul told the Romans the God of peace would shortly bruise Satan under their feet suggests that they (or the church as a whole) were going to witness some aspect of that bruising (Romans 16:20). Satan's ultimate sentence to the lake of fire marks the ultimate completion of the prophecy (Revelation 20:10). The cross began the fulfillment that continues now and will end at the final judgment.

Second, some prophecies are typical. A type is an object lesson, something in the real world that symbolizes and foreshadows the actual, future realization or fulfillment of a particular truth. An antitype is the future realization to which the type points; it is the fulfillment of a picture prophecy. In other words, types are divinely inspired analogies whose salient points not only correspond to but also predict the reality—the antitype, the main topic—of the revelation. Old Testament types fall into three categories: people, things, and events.

Certain people were types not because of their personalities or character traits, but by virtue of their office. Certain things were types by virtue of their function. Certain events were types by virtue of either their agent or their accomplishment. All types are based in historic and actual realities. Many types in the Old Testament already existed in plain view when they were vested with their typical significance. They became object lessons with symbolic significance in the contemporary setting and pointed to the future antitype. The Tabernacle with its structure and ritual illustrates this category of type.

Some types, however, were themselves subjects of prophecy, and this is what sometimes gives the appearance of multiple fulfillments. Isaiah predicted that the Lord would raise up Cyrus, the Persian king, to be His shepherd and His anointed (Isaiah 44:28; 45:1). In fact, Isaiah, one of the richest of messianic prophecies, applies the word "messiah" only to Cyrus. Isaiah, under divine inspiration, uses Cyrus as a type of Christ. Isaiah's point is that God will raise up a powerful leader who will successfully accomplish His purpose in delivering the nation from bondage. In that way the powerful Cyrus, who was himself the subject of prediction, would serve as a picture prophecy of Christ, God's Ideal Leader who will successfully accomplish His purpose in delivering more than Israel from bondage. Many Old Testament prophets predicted the coming of the Day of the Lord. The Old Testament, in fact, uses "Day of the Lord" terminology when foretelling God's judgment on various nations, such as Edom and Babylon. It also projects an eschatological Day that will signal the end of time as we know it. This does not mean that a single prophecy of the Day of the Lord was and will be fulfilled over and over again. Rather, multiple days, each the subject of its own individual prophecy finds single fulfillment. Nevertheless, there is a sense in which every Day of the Lord, which was prophesied and is now past, typifies the final eschatological day. Every judgment of God on the ungodly parallels what God will do in that final day. Types are possible because God controls time.

For a more detailed treatment of the issues of prophecy and typology, consult my discussion in *Beginning at Moses* (2nd edition, 2001). I think I have said enough for now about the nature of history and prophecy to prepare us for the specifics of Daniel's message. Biblical history and prophecy infallibly witness to God's absolute and sovereign control of time and circumstance. Neither could be possible if He were simply a passive spectator of the course of this world. The Bible has revealed absolutely everything that is truly significant for our good: what history records and what prophecy pre-records is what we need to know to rest in the sure operation of His providence. Interpreting time properly requires faith that "His story" is eternally certain and temporally unchangeable. His glory, which includes our redemptive good in Christ, is the glue that holds all the segments of time together and the goal to which all time unfailingly moves–even ours. ⸎

Chapter Four

The Final Four + One

Part One

I t so happens that I am working on this chapter in the middle of March. For me this means that turkey season is just a few weeks away and deer season will not begin for another six long months. For many others, however, March means college basketball. Talk of "March Madness" is inescapable. Daily newspapers print the tournament brackets, providing fans the opportunity to predict what teams will make it to the final four. I am not a basketball fan and have little interest in what so many find thrilling and absorbing during these few weeks–unless, of course, I hear that Michigan has reached the finals. Loyalty to the land of birth applies even to basketball. Go Blue! But all the hype and mania will soon dissipate, and by this time next year what teams survived the road to the final four will have dwindled to inconsequential facts in the ever-growing data base of sports trivia. Basketball's "final four" is not the stuff of history.

Daniel's time chronicle, however, identifies a "final four" of utmost significance to both history and prophecy. Twice, once in chapter 2 and once in chapter 7, Daniel delineates four world empires that begin in his own day and continue one after the other. Unlike the conclusion of the basketball tournament, however, not one of these final four emerges victorious in the end. Another kingdom, immeasurably different from all the others, appears and reigns supreme. So in Daniel's course of time, it is the final four plus one.

Although Daniel does not catalogue every individual nation or political entity between his day and the final day, he marks the progress of the kingdoms of this world with such historic precision and with such prophetic inclusiveness that the inference is unmistakable: God has both purposed and guaranteed the events of time. Kingdoms rise and fall, but only according to God's will. The rise and fall of every earthly kingdom marks the advance of the kingdom of heaven. God's kingdom will come, and His will will be done on earth as certainly as it is in heaven. Daniel's overview of the final four is the *big picture* of how God will achieve His purpose. Everything is under divine control. This is the key component for the theology of time.

THE SETTING OF THE PICTURE

God revealed the big picture of His plan for the nations first to Nebuchadnezzar, the pagan king (Daniel 2), and then to Daniel, His choice servant (Daniel 7). Although their views of the picture differed, the subject of the picture was exactly the same for both. There were two revelations, but only one message; there was something for both the pagan and the believer to learn. The Lord disclosed the first exposure in Nebuchadnezzar's second year, at the beginning of the Neo-Babylonian Empire. The second exposure came into view in the first year of Belshazzar, at the very end of the Neo-Babylonian Empire. At the beginning of the exile, God gave a word to reveal that

He had a plan in operation. On the eve of the exile's end, God gave a word to assure that His plan was operating on schedule.

Since Nebuchadnezzar was a pagan, it is not surprising that he had some problems understanding what God revealed to him via a dream, nor is it surprising that the biblical record, therefore, devotes more space to the circumstances of his dream than to Daniel's vision decades later. Dreams were a common means whereby God revealed truths in the Old Testament dispensation, sometimes even to sinners. Remember, for instance, Pharaoh's dreams that Joseph had to interpret. The sinner could be the conduit through which God communicated, but it required a saint with God-given insight to make sense of it. Even the preliminaries to the revelation of the final four, such as this dream, bring to focus significant truths about the Lord's sovereign rule over time.

Although Nebuchadnezzar did not comprehend the significance of what he had dreamed, he knew it was important. Consequently, he set a standard for his advisors designed to ensure an honest and accurate interpretation. He would trust their explication only if they first repeated to him the details of the dream, which he withheld. "The thing is gone from me: if ye will not make known unto me the dream, with the interpretation thereof, ye shall be cut in pieces, and your houses shall be made a dunghill. But if ye shew the dream, and the interpretation thereof, ye shall receive of me gifts and rewards and great honour" (2:5-6). That "the thing" was gone does not mean that Nebuchadnezzar had forgotten the dream. On the contrary, he remembered it all too well and was not going to take any chance that his advisors might pull a fast one on him; he may have been suspicious that they had done that before (2:9). "The thing" refers to the decree that he had issued which required first the telling of the dream and second its interpretation–or else. My guess is that if the advisors thought that Nebuchadnezzar had really forgotten the dream, they would have been ready to make something up to save themselves and to claim the prize. Their strong protests to the king suggest they understood precisely what was at stake; they recognized that supernatural intervention would be necessary to meet the king's challenge (2:11).

Notwithstanding their wizardry, the soothsaying advisors were incapable of recounting the dream and were thus under sentence of death (2:12). When the executioners reached Daniel, who by default was under the same death sentence, he requested a little time and confidently affirmed that he would satisfy the king's ultimatum (2:16). Daniel and his friends used the time to pray, and God wonderfully answered them by revealing the secret to Daniel. In a vision, Daniel learned what Nebuchadnezzar had dreamed and what it meant (2:19). But before he imparted the contents of the dream to the king, he hinted at the main meaning, first in his prayer of thanksgiving and then in his introduction to Nebuchadnezzar. Before both the heavenly King and the earthly king, Daniel acknowledged that his ability to interpret came from God, who knows absolutely everything (2:22, 28). Daniel discloses in his prayer that God "changeth the times and the seasons: he removeth kings, and setteth up kings" (2:21). Further, he summarizes for Nebuchadnezzar that God is showing him "what shall be in the latter days" (2:28). His assertion sounds very much like Paul's: "For there is no power but of God: the powers that be are ordained of God" (Romans 13:1). This is significant since Daniel said it at the start of the final four, and Paul said it when the last of the final four was in place. Nothing had changed in terms of God's purpose or power. The message of the final four is clear enough: All of time and all that happens in time from the past to the present to the future are the prerogative of the one true, living and only sovereign God. Not even the most powerful kingdoms of earth own their own destinies.

THE PICTURE AND ITS POINT

The Lord conveys this message of His absolute sovereignty in two remarkable apocalyptic revelations–the dream to Nebuchadnezzar and the vision to Daniel. Remember that the apocalyptic genre tends to be rich in the use of symbolic language. Symbolic language is fodder for the imagination, and so long as that imagination is bound and controlled by the emphasis of the context, it is a legitimate and even necessary component in the interpretive process. We will always have to allow for some degree of subjectivity, but the overriding point should command our attention. We should not distract our focus from the main features of the image by trying to match up every small detail with something in the real world. Dogmatism about details may jeopardize the credibility of the big picture if those details prove to be inaccurate. Speculation can never end in certainty, and I do not want my speculations about particular points to compromise certainty about the main point. No speculation is necessary concerning the main point. Daniel told Nebuchadnezzar that what he saw represented four successive kingdoms (2:38-40), and the angelic interpreter told Daniel that what he saw was "four kings, which shall arise out of the earth" (7:17).

God revealed the final four kingdoms to Nebuchadnezzar as a colossus consisting of four metals of decreasing value and increasing strength that was destroyed for no apparent reason by a stone that in turn filled the whole earth. God revealed the same kingdoms to Daniel in a series of four monstrous beasts, each coming out of the churned-up sea, the last of which was destroyed by the Son of Man. Nebuchadnezzar and Daniel saw the same realities through different spectacles and with different emphases. Here I speculate, but perhaps the grandeur of the colossus suggests how man tends to see earthly powers or at least how the kingdoms see themselves, whereas the inhumane monsters underscore what they are in truth as the Lord sees them. Since the four metals from top to bottom correspond to the serial monsters, I will summarize the symbols and identify their referents kingdom by kingdom. Don't let the strange-sounding names and places that I mention put you off from reading. I do not want to get bogged down in the details of Ancient Near Eastern history, but I do want you to see enough of what is now history to be convinced that what is still future is equally certain. Although it may appear that nations come and go according to chance, the fact of the matter is that God is the Lord of history and the course of time belongs to Him.

KINGDOM ONE

THE PICTURE

The description of the giant statue of Nebuchadnezzar's dream focused on four main body parts in descending order: the head, the chest and arms, the stomach and sides (or upper thigh area), and the legs and feet (2:31-33). The head, therefore, represents the first kingdom, and it was made of pure gold. Of all the metals, gold was the most valuable and was most often associated with royal majesty and splendor. Of all the body parts, the head was the command center and was identified, therefore, with absolute authority.

Daniel witnessed four beasts coming one by one out of the sea tossed into chaos by the wind (7:2-3). Most likely, the sea represents the pool of nations from which these predominant powers were going to arise. The wind, that seemingly uncontrollable force of nature controlled only by God (see Psalms 78:26; 107:25; 135:7; and 147:18), suggests that God was setting into motion the tides of circumstance that would bring these nations to the fore. Corresponding to the statue's golden head was the odd-appearing lion of Daniel's vision. This lion had the wings of an eagle, at least for a while. The wings were plucked off, and the lion stood erect, possessing not only human posture but also a human heart. The imagery of the lion and eagle is fairly clear. In ancient as well as modern times the lion and the eagle symbolized regal power and authority. The lion was the king of beasts (Proverbs 30:30), proverbial for its strength (Judges 14:18), courage (2 Samuel 17:10), and boldness (Proverbs 28:1); the eagle was the monarch of birds, known for its vigor (Psalm 103:5), swiftness (Jeremiah 48:40), and fierceness (Deuteronomy 28:49; Job 9:26). Thus, like the golden head, the winged lion was a vivid symbol of royal majesty and splendor. The humanizing of the beast is a bit more mysterious, but it obviously pictures a drastic transformation that occurs in the kingdom.

THE POINT

The Scripture explicitly defines the point of the first picture and thereby provides the clue and the starting place for interpreting the components that follow. Daniel boldly told Nebuchadnezzar, "Thou art this head of gold" (2:38). Immediately preceding that interpretive declaration, Daniel extolled the greatness of Nebuchadnezzar's kingship and kingdom while making it clear that the God of heaven had given him "a kingdom, power, and strength, and glory" (2:37). Calling him "a king of kings" was a way of stating the superlative: Nebuchadnezzar was the greatest king. The images of the golden head and the eagle-winged lion portrayed Nebuchadnezzar and his Neo-Babylonian Empire well.

The facts of history verify the vividness of the picture. The Neo-Babylonian Empire was short-lived but glorious, and Nebuchadnezzar, the first of its kings, was without parallel in the regime that followed. After the Assyrian capital, Nineveh, fell to a Babylonian-Medo coalition in 612 B.C., a power-struggle ensued over control of territories previously under Assyrian domination. A treaty between the Babylonians and the Medes settled issues and set borders for these allies, but diplomacy failed between the Babylonians and the Egyptians, particularly over the region of Syria. Nabopollassar sent his son, the crown prince Nebuchadnezzar, to secure Syria before Pharaoh Neco II could. This, by the way, is the Neco who killed Josiah at Megiddo when the good but militarily imprudent king of Judah tried to prevent the Egyptian from making inroads into Syria (2 Kings 23:29). That tragedy occurred in 609 B.C., but things came to a head in 605 B.C. when Neco and Nebuchadnezzar collided at Carchemish on the Euphrates, near the border of what is now Syria and Turkey. The Babylonian forces were victorious, and the Battle of Carchemish marked the beginning of the Neo-Babylonian kingdom. About the same time, Nabopollassar died, making Nebuchadnezzar not only the conquering general but also the head of the new world kingdom. Remember that it was partly in celebration of this victory that Nebuchadnezzar returned home with the spoils of conquest, part of which included Daniel. The beginning of the empire marked the first stage in Judah's exile; this was all part of God's plan.

The kingdom flourished under the headship of Nebuchadnezzar. His building activity in the kingdom is well known, and his famous hanging gardens became one of the wonders of the ancient world. From a purely human perspective Nebuchadnezzar's boast was warranted: "Is not this great Babylon, that I have built for the house of the kingdom by the might of my power, and for the honour of my majesty?" (4:30). Without dispute, Nebuchadnezzar elevated Babylon to be the queen of all kingdoms. His power appeared to be absolute as he reigned from 605–562 B.C. Notwithstanding the glory Nebuchadnezzar achieved for his kingdom, it did not last long. Within twenty-five years of his death, his kingdom–the first of the final four–fell to kingdom two.

Identifying the head of gold is easy enough since Daniel did it for us. However, we are on our own in attempting to discover the meaning of the part of Daniel's vision picturing the drastic transformation in the kingdom. I believe that there are two distinct parts and two separate referents involved in this transformation. First, I think that the part of the transformation involving the humanizing of the lion refers to Nebuchadnezzar personally. Remember that as Daniel looked at the lion, it was made to "stand upon the feet as a man, and man's heart was given to it" (7:4). Before Daniel told Nebuchadnezzar that he was the head of gold, he told him that "the God of heaven hath given thee a kingdom, power, and strength, and glory" (2:37).

Apparently, Nebuchadnezzar got the point that he was the head of gold, but it did not sink in that God had given him his authority (see 4:30 again). Sometime after his kingdom reached its elevated status, God gave Nebuchadnezzar another dream that Daniel, reluctantly, had to interpret for him (chapter 4). I will examine the details of this dream and interpretation later, but here I want us to see simply how this dream and its fulfillment relate to the lion's transformation. God was going to humiliate the proud king "to the intent that the living may know that the most High ruleth in the kingdom of men, and giveth it to whomsoever he will, and setteth up over it the basest of men" (4:17). Ironically, God put a man's heart into the beast by putting a beast's heart into a man (4:16). This time Nebuchadnezzar got the point. His confession of the absolute sovereignty and power of God is classic; it sums up nicely the whole message of Daniel. Nebuchadnezzar confessed a good theology of time.

> I blessed the most High, and I praised and honoured him that liveth for ever, whose dominion is an everlasting dominion, and his kingdom is from generation to generation: And all the inhabitants of the earth are reputed as nothing: and he doeth according to his will in the army of heaven and among the inhabitants of the earth: and none can stay his hand....Now I Nebuchadnezzar praise and extol and honour the King of heaven, all whose works are truth, and his ways judgment: and those that walk in pride he is able to abase. (4:34-35)

The extent of Nebuchadnezzar's change is disputed, but the orthodoxy of the confession suggests a genuine and spiritual change of heart. I believe that the humanizing of the lion symbolized the gracious conversion of the pagan king.

Second, I suggest that the part of the transformation involving the plucking of the wings from the lion refers to the weakening of the kingdom as a whole. None of Nebuchadnezzar's successors shared his charisma or abilities. For the names of his successors whose incompetence sabotaged the kingdom, consult the chart "The Times of Daniel (+ or -)" in the appendices. The only names recognizable from the Bible are Amel-Marduk and Belshazzar. Amel-Marduk is the Evil-merodach (the man of Marduk) who granted amnesty to Jehoichin, the exiled Judean king (2 Kings 25:27-30). He was not particularly significant in Babylonian history and, after a brief reign, was deposed by his brother-in-law, Neriglissar. Were it not for his kind gesture to Jehoichin, he would probably not have made it into the biblical history. The biblical record did not regard any of the following kings to be important and ignored them all until Belshazzar, the last of the Babylonian regime (mentioned in Daniel 5, 7, and 8). The point of sacred history is that God raised up the Babylonians, and He caused them to fall as well. Mentioning the first and the last makes the point sufficiently. Belshazzar, whose historicity was long suspect among critics, was co-regent with his father Nabonidus. The secular Greek historian Herodotus (fifth century B.C.) did not mention Belshazzar, so biblically skeptical critics were inclined to take his word over Daniel's. When some cuneiform tablets dating to the time of Nabonidus and mentioning Belshazzar as co-regent in Babylon surfaced, even the skeptics had to admit that Daniel was right after all. This just illustrates again what we've already noted about the nature of history and historians: Herodotus did not know everything, and biblical history is always correct.

The secular records do, however, bear witness to a kingdom just waiting to fall–its wings were plucked. The *Nabonidus Chronicle* from Babylon and the *Cyrus Cylinder* from Persia tell essentially the same story of Babylon's fall. In 539 B.C. the city of Babylon, and consequently the kingdom, fell to the Persians virtually "without a shot being fired." Nabonidus had been a high-ranking official under Nebuchadnezzar; after a series of weak rulers, he was able to secure the throne through some political maneuvering. But his status as a devotee of the moon god Sin whose "domain" was in northern Mesopotamia caused a rift with the priests of Marduk, the patron deity of Babylon. The priests of Marduk regarded him as the heretic king. It was his frequent absence from Babylon due to religious, diplomatic, and economic reasons that necessitated his appointment of Belshazzar as co-regent to administer the affairs of state in Babylon. Unquestionably, Cyrus had some spies who learned of the civil and religious unrest, and he utilized the intelligence reports masterfully. Claiming to be called by Marduk to liberate the city, Cyrus was received with open arms. The fact that at the moment of the city's surrender Belshazzar was celebrating adds to the irony. Golden Babylon had lost its glory. But there is more to the story; there are three more kingdoms.

Kingdom Two

The Picture

The chest and arms picture the second kingdom, and they were made of silver (2:32). Although not as valuable as gold, silver was nonetheless a precious metal that along with gold functioned as a standard of wealth and commerce recognized throughout the ancient world. The chest and arms were parts of the body associated with strength and activity. So proportionately, this kingdom might not be as majesty as the first, but it would be powerful and resourceful. Daniel, in fact, told Nebuchadnezzar that this next kingdom would be inferior (2:39). The second beast of Daniel's vision conveyed the same idea. Daniel saw a bear with one side elevated over the other with three ribs in its mouth (7:5). A bear, although less majestic than a lion, is larger and stronger and renowned for its ferocity (2 Samuel 17:8). At the very least, the detail of the three ribs hanging out of the bear's mouth pictures it in the process of devouring its prey.

THE POINT

Since Daniel explicitly identified Nebuchadnezzar as the golden head and the rest of the image as the kingdoms to follow him, it is not difficult to ascertain the meaning of the lopsided bear. The kingdom of the Medes and Persians with Cyrus at the head followed Babylon. This is itself amazing evidence of the Lord's control of the whole course of events. Years before Babylon even rose to power, Isaiah had predicted that God would "stir up the Medes against them" (Isaiah 13:17) and that "Babylon, the glory of kingdoms, the beauty of the Chaldees' excellency, shall be as when God overthrew Sodom and Gomorrah" (Isaiah 13:19). Recall that about two hundred years before the fact, Isaiah had also predicted that God would raise up from the north a "messiah" named Cyrus to deliver His people from the Babylonian exile (Isaiah 44:28; 45:1). Although in separate contexts, Isaiah linked the Medes with the Persians. What Isaiah prophesied from a distance, Daniel prophesied near at hand and then witnessed with his own eyes. Isaiah's distant prophecies and Daniel's near prophecies correspond precisely. Daniel's symbolism shows how God's plan was coming together.

The facts of history demonstrate the accuracy of Isaiah's prophecies and explain the salient features of Daniel's symbolism. According to both the Babylonian and the Persian accounts, Cyrus conquered Babylon with little effort. The surrender of Babylon to Cyrus in 539 B.C. marked the beginning of the Medo-Persian Empire that was geographically more extensive than Babylon and chronologically longer in duration, extending for about two hundred years. Babylon's fall was the dramatic transition from the golden head to the silver chest.

However, some factors antecedent to that climactic event help to explain the peculiar features of the lumbering, lopsided bear. The story really begins at a point even before the commencement of Nebuchadnezzar's golden reign. Previously, a coalition between Babylon and Media had led to the fall of Nineveh in 612 B.C. After that victory, the allies agreed on their borders and went about the business of establishing their respective kingdoms. Toward the end of the Babylonian regime, a shift of power was taking place within the Median kingdom. Media, the northern part of the kingdom just south of the Caspian Sea, had been the center of power most of the duration of Babylon's kingdom, but that changed with the appearance of Cyrus. He was from Persia, the southern part of the kingdom just east of the Persian Gulf. When Cyrus defeated Astyages, the Mede, in 549 B.C., the Persian bloc assumed prominence. The Medes and Persians shared a similar culture, so this did not prove a difficult arrangement. I think that the bear of Daniel's vision was lopsided—one side elevated over the other—to picture the supremacy of the Persians over the Medes in this otherwise single kingdom.

What happened next explains the three ribs. Not long after the establishment of the Medo-Persian union, Cyrus defeated Croessus of Lydia, what we now know as western Turkey. This victory was significant for a couple of reasons. First, it effectively broke an alliance between Lydia, Babylon and Egypt, and thus set the stage for the fall of the whole region to the Persians. Some interpreters specify the three ribs between the bear's teeth as Lydia, Babylon and Egypt, the three principal powers whose subjugation was vital to the consolidation of the empire. That reading is certainly feasible. If not alluding to these three powers specifically, the ribs hanging out of the mouth may more generally picture the insatiable appetite of the constantly prowling bear as it devoured anything and everything in sight. Lydia, Babylon and Egypt were all west of Persia. In all likelihood, there were some ribs for the bear to gnaw on to the east as well. We know that the empire extended eastward as far as India (see Esther 1:1). Be sure to consult the maps in the appendices to see the borders of each of these four kingdoms.

Second, Cyrus's defeat of Croessus was significant because it marked Persia's first contact with Greece and also illustrated a policy of toleration that eventually characterized Cyrus's leadership philosophy. The *Cyrus Cylinder*, which records the surrender of Babylon, also delineates Cyrus's policy of lenience and essential toleration of divergent cultures and religions that became part of his political domain. It was this policy, by the way, which allowed the exiles of Judah to return to Palestine according to God's will. From the biblical perspective, this is the most important implication of the policy, but unquestionably, it also did much to help consolidate the empire, particularly in its infancy. It appears that Cyrus was already operating according to this fundamental principle of government even before his decrees to repatriate all of Babylon's exiles. Lydia neighbored Greece and had been greatly influenced by Greek ideas and culture. Notwithstanding the degree of dissimilarity between the Greek and Persian cultures, Cyrus was lenient in his dealings with Croessus. But this first contact with Greece that Cyrus met with sufferance foreshadowed conflict to come. In the end, the Greeks would be Persia's downfall. Kingdom three was on the way.

There is far too much Persian history to consider here, but I think we have surveyed enough to get the point of Daniel's vividly precise pictures. Old Testament history runs out before the end of the Persian Empire. The post-exilic books, both prophetic (Haggai and Zechariah) and historic (Chronicles, Ezra, Nehemiah, Esther), mention by name the Persian kings whose administrations had direct bearing on the progress of redemptive history: Cyrus, Darius I, Xerxes (Ahasuerus), and Artaxerxes I. God raised them up and used them well for His own glorious purpose.

KINGDOM THREE

THE PICTURE

The third kingdom is represented by the bronze torso of Nebuchadnezzar's dream (2:32) and by the four-winged, four-headed leopard of Daniel's vision (7:6). The picture is starting to get stranger. The word translated "brass" in the Authorized Version can refer to either pure copper or bronze, an alloy of copper and lead. The association of bronze with strength (Job 6:12), warfare (1 Samuel 17:5-6), and judgment (Judges 16:21; Jeremiah 52:11) makes it, rather than copper, the more likely choice for the metal composing the stomach and sides (or upper thighs). Although not a precious metal like gold and silver, it was functionally stronger and more utilitarian. The odd-looking leopard is more mysterious. The Old Testament does not often mention leopards, but when it does, it focuses on the predatory nature of the beast (Isaiah 11:6; Jeremiah 5:6; Hosea 13:7). I have watched enough of the Discovery Channel to know something about leopards. They certainly have the strength to dispatch their prey quickly. What leopards may lack in stamina, they make up with speed. The leopard stalks and then lies in ambush until the opportunity arises to pounce swiftly on its prey. But I have never seen on the Discovery Channel the kind of leopard that Daniel describes: It had four wings and four heads. Although the presence of wings may do nothing more than enhance the notion of swiftness, the multiple heads suggest a division of command. Four heads on a single body would indicate four command centers and the consequent potential for rivalry and competition. That the number of wings equals the number of heads probably means that those two oddities are linked in significance. That seems easy enough!

THE POINT

The third kingdom was Greece, and as Daniel explained to Nebuchadnezzar this third kingdom would "rule over all the earth" (2:39). That this kingdom would be strong, swift, opportunistic, and segmented is clear enough from the symbolism. But we have an advantage over Daniel in that enough time has passed to help us interpret the details. Daniel knew the basic facts; we can add the names.

The conflict between Persia and Greece (kingdoms two and three) stretches back as far as the time of Darius I, whose latter years were pestered by tensions and military skirmishes with the Greeks. In 490 B.C. Darius suffered a significant defeat at the Battle of Marathon. His successor, Xerxes (the Ahasuerus of Esther), was obsessed with avenging that defeat. But over and over again, the Greek forces frustrated his efforts and fueled his obsession. The decimation of his naval fleet at Salamis in 480 B.C. forced him home in humiliation. Although more than a hundred years remained for the Persian Empire, to borrow Belshazzar's portent, "the handwriting was on the wall." The Greeks were coming.

Troubles of one sort or another mark the waning years of any regime. That's what makes them wane, and troubles certainly plagued Persia. Insurrections in Egypt and parts of Asia Minor diverted attention from the ongoing Greek nemesis. While the last Persian kings were successively trying to put out fires of rebellion throughout the empire, Philip of Macedonia (359-336 B.C.) consolidated power over the Greek states, creating a base of operation for the foreign campaigns that were on the near horizon. When he was assassinated, Alexander, his son, ascended to this base of power. The leopard was in place and ready to go.

The conquests of Alexander the Great (336-323 B.C.) are legendary. Motivated philosophically by a Pan-Hellenistic (everything Greek) ideal and vindictively by anti-Persian spite, he embarked on his famous campaign. In 334 B.C. he crossed the Hellespont and in the following year defeated Darius III at Issus (on Turkey's coast northeast of Cyrpus) in one of the most decisive battles in world history. Darius retreated only to meet Alexander again in 331 B.C at Arbela on the Tigris, Persia's last stand. Alexander then led his troops to Babylon, Susa and Persepolis, the Persian capital, where he ruthlessly avenged the Persian atrocities committed against the Greeks. Alexander marched eastward, meeting virtually no resistance on his way to the Indus River. The empire was in place. Then as legend has it, he wept because there were no more worlds to conquer. He died in Babylon, a young man in his early thirties. Alexander swiftly inaugurated Greek rule. Whereas his Persian predecessors officially governed with a "live and let live" tolerance, Alexander's agenda was to unite his empire under the flag of Hellenism (i.e., devotion to all things Greek). Although he did not live long enough to see the full implementation of his dream, his successors shared the dream, and the agenda of Hellenization held sway.

What happened after Alexander's death explains the oddities of the four wings and four heads that grew out of the leopard. Some interpreters link the "fours" to Daniel's statement that this kingdom would "rule over all the earth" (2:39). That is, the third kingdom's dominion would be universal, at least hyperbolically, since "four" designates the "four corners" of the earth. Although that is true enough, the facts of history correlate with the image enough to make me think that in this context four actually means four. Though not without some political maneuvering, the administration of the expansive empire was ultimately divided among four of Alexander's generals: Lysimachus, Antipater, Ptolemy, and Seleucus. Lysimachus governed Thrace and Bithynia (the regions sandwiched between the Aegean and Black Seas, i.e., Asia Minor). Antipater and then Cassander commanded Macedonia and Greece. Ptolemy controlled Palestine and Egypt. Seleucus ruled Syria eastward to India. The empire remained loosely intact, but four heads made conflict inevitable: Each wanted to be the biggest of the heads.

From the perspective of biblical history, the competition between the Seleucids and the Ptolemies is the most important one because Israel was caught in the middle. The Seleucids, perhaps more than any of the other heads, attempted to reunify the empire. Daniel provides by prediction some amazing details about the Seleucids and their quest to usurp what had been assigned to the Ptolemies. We will consider the details of that part of the picture a bit later. For now, I want us to see the big picture. At this point, Daniel does not delineate any specifics about the four-headed leopard, only that its dominion was received, not achieved (7:6). God ordained the leopard and every one of its heads. The influence of Hellenistic culture and language that accompanied the Greek conquest would survive the political regime and would have weighty implications for the sure progress of redemptive history. For instance, with the widespread use of the Greek language, a vehicle was in place to disseminate the gospel message swiftly throughout the civilized world, both through the written word of Scripture and the spoken word of preaching. Paul could preach from Jerusalem to Rome without ever going to language school. The Lord used the bizarre leopard to accomplish His purpose.

KINGDOM FOUR

THE PICTURE

The picture of the fourth kingdom, as portrayed in both Nebuchadnezzar's dream and Daniel's vision, is the most complex. On the colossus, the legs and feet represent the fourth domain. The legs are iron, and the feet are a composite of iron and clay (2: 33). Although iron was not a precious metal, it was, nonetheless, a valuable commodity in the ancient world. It produced durable tools and potent weapons. The Scripture associates iron with invincible weaponry (Joshua 17:16; Judges 1:19), power (Job 40:18), savagery (Amos 1:3), harsh affliction (Deuteronomy 4:20; 28:48), obstinacy (Isaiah 48:4), indestructibility (Jeremiah 15:12), and sovereign severity (Psalm 2:9). Clay is the very opposite. Depending on its form, clay is as fragile as iron is unbreakable, or as pliable as iron is unbendable. It was a common commodity; the most ordinary and mundane utensils of daily life were made of clay. Consequently, it fittingly pictures weakness (Job 13:12; Psalm 31:12) and dispensability (Jeremiah 18). Thus, it is ironically incongruous that iron and clay are combined. I don't know whether the mixture consisted of a clay lump with iron fragments peppered in to mold the feet or simply if clay was inserted between the iron toes. At the very least, this colossal statue stands on extraordinarily precarious footing.

The first three beasts of Daniel's vision were strange, but there was something about them that Daniel could recognize. The lion had wings, but it was clearly a lion. The bear was lopsided, but it was clearly a bear. The leopard had multiple wings and heads, but it was clearly a leopard. Daniel had no point of reference for the fourth beast; differing from all the preceding monsters (7:7), it was not like anything that he had seen before. All he could do was to describe its horrific features and behavior that were dreadful, terrible, and strong (7:7). He focused on the iron teeth that devoured whatever they could and on the feet that trampled whatever the beast didn't eat. The beast also had ten horns, which after a while were joined by another little horn, which in turn removed three of the ten horns. To add to the strangeness, this usurping horn could see and talk (7:7-8). We have our work cut out for us as we try to think through this one.

THE POINT

On the surface some elements of the picture are clear and easily identifiable if we have been correct in the preceding analysis. Starting with Nebuchadnezzar's Neo-Babylonian kingdom, we have simply followed history's progression from Babylon to Persia to Greece. Following that progression, Rome would come next. Tomes have been written on the rise and fall of the Roman Empire, and it is not my intention to add to them. I just want to note a couple of things particularly relevant to the rise of this kingdom that was in place in the fullness of time at Christ's first advent and, as we shall see, will still be in place in the next fullness of time when Christ returns.

The beginning of Rome's rise to power is hard to pinpoint; the difficulty in part relates to Greece's pluralistic order. Not long after 200 B.C., Rome started annexing Greek territories bit by bit, subduing most of Macedonia and Greece by about 145 B.C. Pompey conquered the Seleucid domain west of the Tigris River, including Palestine and Jerusalem, in 63 B.C. By 31 B.C., Egypt had become a province of Rome. So if we calculate the duration of the Greek Empire from the time of Alexander to the Roman occupation of Egypt, it lasted for about three hundred years. Yet who knows exactly when to date the beginning of the Roman Empire? It depended on location. Nevertheless, even if the date is uncertain, the method of Roman conquest is not. Rome's quest for power was marked by violence, and thus it corresponds vividly to iron's ability to break (2:40) and the beast's ability to devour and stomp (7:7). Surveying Rome's innovative military tactics and state-of-the-art arsenal is beyond our concern except to note how those strategies and weaponry combined to give a realistic guarantee of victory in every battle. The Roman legions were virtually invincible.

Nebuchadnezzar's colossus had "feet and toes, part of potter's clay, and part of iron" (2:41). Although Daniel does not say so explicitly, I would be surprised if there were not ten toes altogether. Ten toes are normal; the statue had a complete set of toes. Daniel's monster had ten horns. I think that the ten toes and the ten horns correspond, although not in the way some suggest. Here's the point. Just as the statue had a complete set of toes, so the monster's having ten horns symbolizes the totality of its power. Throughout Scripture, horns represent power (e.g., Psalm 18:2; Zechariah 1:18-21), and the number ten seems to represent completeness. So rather than trying to pick out ten specific kings–one for each toe or horn–we would do better to apply the image to the whole of empire. During the height of the empire, Rome ruled supremely. Roman law was backed by Roman might. No one could "mess with" Rome and get away with it. Remember what happened to Jerusalem in A.D. 70.

Notwithstanding the immense puissance of this fourth kingdom, it was destined to be replaced by yet another. In God's purpose, one more kingdom would follow the final four. The remaining details of Nebuchadnezzar's dream and Daniel's vision concern the coming of the kingdom of all kingdoms, the kingdom of the Christ of God. Given how much history we have had to wade through, I think it best to take a break and devote the next chapter to the deep prophecies that are before us. Keep in mind that what we have considered in historical terms was future from Daniel's perspective. Although I have only highlighted some general facts, I want us to be impressed with how accurately and precisely the prophecies were fulfilled. God could reveal the future because He controls time. And let's not forget to make the personal application: He controls our times. Daniel proves it. ⤵

CHAPTER FIVE

THE FINAL FOUR + ONE

PART TWO

Kingdoms come, and kingdoms go. The legs and feet of Nebuchadnezzar's dream and the monstrous beast of Daniel's vision represent the final kingdom in the series of four that extend from the latter part of the 7th century B.C. to the last days of time as we know it. The rise of kingdom four is not the end of the story. It, like all of its predecessors, must give way to another. But its successor will be a kingdom unlike any the world has ever known: It will rise, but it will never fall. It is to the genesis of this everlasting kingdom that all time is headed. Just as certainly as moment follows moment and time marches on, this kingdom will come. The one that follows the final four is the Kingdom of our God and Christ.

Both the colossus and the peculiar beast parade give way to the last of all the kingdoms without interruption. Remember that prophecy often links distant epoch events into single predictive contexts. In a single utterance, the prophet makes multiple predictions, connecting them without reference to time intervals. Although the Rome that rose to power as Daniel's fourth kingdom declined from power sometime in the 5th century A.D., it nonetheless seems to be the part of the statue that sustains the final blow and the beast in Daniel's vision that is slain. There is something about that kingdom that continues until the end. Using quintessential prophetic perspective, Daniel telescoped the rise and the fall of this kingdom without any hint of the time distance. What he saw as the rise of kingdom four was hundreds of years in the future from his vantage point but past from our point of view, and what he saw as the kingdom's fall has yet to be fulfilled. In juxtaposing the rise and fall of Rome, he overlooked much of what is now history and quite probably much of what is still future. Notwithstanding the prophetic silence about the "in-between" events, we can be certain that none of them will jeopardize the already ordained outcome. I think, in fact, that Scripture's leaving out the "in-between" information intensifies the certainty of the outcome and generates the assurance that everything in between must purposefully contribute to the climax. So even though I don't know exactly where my time fits into the big picture of God's plan, I know that it fits.

Knowing that it must fit, however, raises a potential problem–making it fit. My wife loves to work on jigsaw puzzles. Often she has one in progress on a table in the corner of our den. I don't know if this is cheating or not, but she usually has the lid of the box on the table with a picture of what she is trying to put together from all the little divergently shaped pieces. I do not share her patience, but sometimes as I walk by the table I will take a quick look and find what I think is a match between one of the pieces and one of the holes in the fragmented picture. It seems to be the right color and more or less the right configuration, and so I make my contribution to her project. When I force the piece into place doing my best to make it fit, she invariably tells me to leave it alone and find something else to do.

To me it was close enough, but it didn't really fit. (Sometimes when I walk by, I hide a piece or two, but that's a different story.) The way I work with jigsaw puzzles is the way too many tend to work with prophecy. Zeal for fulfillment sometimes creates the temptation to draw from the table of current events and force newspaper items into the big puzzle-picture of prophecy. I would not begin to guess how many commentaries have been written or how many sermons have been preached that now contain the marred fragments of pieces of news that in the moment seemed to be close enough to fit. I wonder how many antichrists have been named over the years, only now to be long dead and forgotten. When my puzzle-patient wife finds the right piece, it always fits in place without being forced. When it fits, it fits. The fulfillment of prophecy is always unmistakably certain.

As I am writing this chapter, war is raging in Iraq–the very place where the final four began. The attention of the world is right where it was in Daniel's day. I have to wonder whether this is just another divinely purposed "in-between" event or whether this is indeed a piece in the specifically revealed prophetic puzzle. I tend to have more discipline with prophecy than I do with my wife's puzzles, so I will resist the temptation to force its place in the big picture. We must be cautious not to force interpretations and identifications by speculation. There is a difference between interpreting current events in the light of the Bible and interpreting the Bible in the light of current events. I must always bring God's Word to bear on current events, but I don't want what may prove to be my zealous mistakes to jeopardize confidence in the sure Word of God. However, when from time to time we see things that look close enough to fit, we should be encouraged that things are getting more and more into place. Without doubt I can say that what is happening in Iraq and the Middle East today brings us closer to the fall of the fourth kingdom than we have ever been before. Without doubt I can also say that what is happening today as I write on the morning of April 2, 2003, or for that matter what is happening on whatever day you may be reading, is part of the unimpedable, eternally determined plan of God. Faith in God and His Word assures us that everything is under control.

So as we consider the yet-to-be-fulfilled elements of the dream-image and vision-beasts, we should remember what we have learned from the fulfilled elements: The fulfillment confirmed and clarified the symbols. Daniel was able to see the shape of the big picture; we are able to add the details of actual dates, names, and places. The field has been leveled, however, as we look at the future. Like Daniel, we will be able to see the shape of the big picture without being able to identify dates, names, and places. Our inability to date, name, or locate specifics does not affect the certainty of the fulfillment. When these prophecies are fulfilled, the details will become clear. When it fits, it fits. In the meantime, all of the purposes of prophecy should be operative–to glorify God, to instill confidence for daily living, to increase desire for God's will, and to produce purity. With this in mind, I want to ponder the fall of the fourth kingdom and the inauguration of the forever kingdom.

THE CONTINUATION OF THE OLD

Although some interpreters see the end as involving a revived Roman Empire, neither Nebuchadnezzar's dream nor Daniel's vision suggests anything about a revival. A revival implies a rebirth of something defunct, a new beginning. The fourth kingdom begins once and does not become defunct until it meets an irreversible and catastrophic end. The fourth kingdom continues without interruption–howbeit with significant alterations–until Christ comes to set up the everlasting kingdom. It rises once; it falls once–at least according to biblical data. It is interesting, also, that many who speak in terms of a revived Roman Empire seem to focus their eschatological vision on Europe as though Europe was the only domain of the Roman Empire. Remember that while each of the four kingdoms had distinctive borders, they all shared some territory. (See again the maps in the appendices.) At the heart of each successive hegemony was Nebuchadnezzar's kingdom: the main of what we now call the Middle East, from Iraq right over to Israel, the hotbed of world tension and crisis today. I don't think we should forget this part of it. The little horn that will rise up among the ten horns could theoretically, in keeping with biblical parameters, come from between the Tigris and Euphrates as well as from some European federation. As I write, only God knows.

There is one more issue that complicates our interpretation of the fall of the fourth kingdom. I sincerely believe that my overall analysis of the statue and divergent creatures is correct in that it sees the progression of kingdoms from Babylon to Rome. One kingdom seems to replace the other. Yet in the end, even though the final blow hits the feet, which are a specific part of the fourth kingdom, the entire image as a whole is broken in pieces–"the iron, the brass, the clay, the silver, and the gold" (2:45). In the end, after the fourth beast is slain, the others remained "for a season and time" (7:12). So it seems that more is involved than just the historic identifications. There is a sense in which the details of the dream and vision represent the totality of human government, regardless of time and location. That totality takes many forms and will one day in its entirety cease to be. Therefore, the image, composed specifically of Babylon, Persia, Greece and Rome, by metonymy stood for every gentile kingdom. Similarly, by brachylogy (a partial list to represent the whole) the series of specifically identifiable beasts also represents the totality of human government. God's obvious control of the parts is evidence of His control over the whole: His Kingdom has no rival. In this sense, America is part of prophecy after all. But having said this, I do believe that the special focus of the end is again on the regions and regimes specified in the dream and vision.

This has been a bit complicated. I hope you are still with me as we try to focus in on the big picture. My concern for now is that we don't over-speculate and that we don't become overly dogmatic regarding the specifics of our interpretation. Some may regard this as weakness of conviction, but I think it rather to be hermeneutical wisdom. So with this caveat, let's think through what Daniel reveals about the situation of the fourth kingdom as it nears its end. Two foci stand out: the state of the kingdom and the ascendancy of the final tyrant.

THE STATE OF THE KINGDOM

Heterogeneity, upheaval, and disunity mark the final state of the kingdom. In his interpretation of the dream to Nebuchadnezzar, Daniel directed attention away from the legs to the feet and toes and explained the significance (2:41-43). The obvious transition from the single composition of the iron legs to the amalgam of the feet indicated an alteration in the kingdom. That the toes were partly iron and partly clay meant that part of the kingdom would be strong and part would be fragile. Efforts to unify the divergent parts would fail because iron and clay just don't mix.

More details come into focus in Daniel's vision of the fourth beast. At first sight, the beast had ten horns, representing unified power (7: 7). However, as Daniel was considering the ten horns, he witnessed a transition (7:8): The beast was in a process of development. A little horn sprang up and uprooted three of the horns that were already there. The horns (i.e., the power) then become divided: Seven remain intact; one, having usurped three, gains prominence. Daniel's interpreter explained that "the ten horns out of this kingdom are ten kings that shall arise: and another shall rise after them; and he shall be diverse from the first, and he shall subdue three kings" (7:24). I think that the correspondence between the ten horns and the ten kings is simply a way of expressing the initial unity that characterized the "iron" stage of the kingdom. It is a picture of completeness–a king for a horn. It all fits. I would rather leave it there than to name specific kings–either past, present, or future. Clearly, though, that unity is eventually disrupted, with a portion of the previously indivisible kingdom becoming predominant.

Even without the details of names, dates, and places, we can get a pretty good idea of the state of world politics in the closing days of the dispensation of human government. It will be a world in disarray and chaos, out of which a ruler will arise who attempts to bring some unity. The situation of the last days as suggested by Daniel sounds to me very much like what Paul describes in 2 Thessalonians 2. The apostle refers to a falling away or rebellion that precedes the revelation of one he calls "the man of sin" and "son of perdition." I believe that Daniel's little usurping horn is Paul's man of sin, and we will get to him directly. But Paul also says that the appearing of the man of sin follows the removal of a restraining influence. "And now ye know what withholdeth that he might be revealed in his time. For the mystery of iniquity doth already work: only he who now letteth will let, until he be taken out of the way" (2 Thessalonians 2:6-7). The word that the Authorized Version translates as "withholdeth" and "letteth" means to restrain or to hold in check. The identity of the restraining influence that holds things in check is a matter of disputed interpretation. Some see it as a reference to the Holy Spirit. On condition that we do not equate the ceasing of a particular ministry of the Holy Spirit with the "physical" removal of the Holy Spirit from the earth via the rapture, I suppose I have no real problem with this view. Regardless of where we place the rapture on the eschatological timeline, we must be careful not to confine the presence and the ministry of the Holy Spirit to within the church collectively or Christians individually. That would be a huge mistake. Others see the restrainer as a reference to the restricting operation of government (see Romans 13:1-7; Titus 3:1; 1 Peter 2:13-14, 17). I am inclined to agree, although not dogmatically, with this second interpretation, and it seems to accord with Daniel's picture of the state of the final kingdom. Out of upheaval and chaos comes some attempt at unification by the little horn. Regardless of how we specifically identify the restrainer, one thing is clear: It is God who removes it and thus sets in place the circumstances that He has ordained. I know I've said it before, but God is in control.

THE ASCENDANCY OF THE FINAL TYRANT

Although Nebuchadnezzar's colossus provides a general picture of the state of the final kingdom immediately preceding its fall, it does not supply any specific information about the final tyrant. Daniel's vision of the fourth beast, on the other hand, introduces a figure whose career comes to focus in even greater detail in subsequent visions. Daniel's first revelation of this character was the commandeering little horn (7:8, 11, 20-21, 25). Five particulars stand out. (1) It would rule only a portion of what was the fourth kingdom. The horn is not the head of a one-world government; it subdues only three of the ten horns. The seven remaining horns are not part of his jurisdiction. (2) It would have eyes and a mouth speaking great things against the Most High. (3) It would wage war against the saints with apparent success for a predetermined duration ("a time and times and the dividing of time"). This most plausibly calculates to three and one-half years or forty-two months, a highly charged prophetic period of time. (4) It would attempt to change times and laws. I think that in part this will involve the creation of a new calendar reckoning devoid of any Christian reference. My guess is that it will go far beyond even current trends to refer to B.C. dates (before Christ) as B.C.E. (before the Common Era). (5) It would be destroyed, especially because of what it said. I am going to postpone discussing the significance of all this to the next chapter, where I will consider in detail the opposition leveled against the accomplishing of God's plan. This character, the little horn, climaxes that opposition.

Suffice it to say for now that I would identify this little horn with the seven-headed and ten-horned beast of Revelation 13. Like Daniel's little horn, John's beast will speak blasphemies against God, will wage war with the saints for forty-two months (i.e., a time and times and the dividing of time), and will enjoy worldwide influence. The parallels are too close to be coincidental. I believe that both Daniel's little horn and John's beast are to identified with Paul's man of sin, "Who opposeth and exalteth himself above all that is called God...whom the

Lord shall consume with the spirit of his mouth, and shall destroy with the brightness of his coming" (2 Thessalonians 2:4, 8). Let's call him the Antichrist. All that we need to see for now is that this tyrant rises and falls in God's timing. The Antichrist himself will be an unwitting dupe in the accomplishing of God's will. He marks the final stage of the final kingdom.

THE INAUGURATION OF THE NEW

The kingdom that follows the final four is infinitely different from any and every other government. It is an ideal Kingdom because it is ruled by an ideal King. The Spirit of the Lord spoke through David, the sweet psalmist of Israel: "He that ruleth over men must be just, ruling in the fear of God" (2 Samuel 23:1-3). David said of this ideal King that "He shall have dominion also from sea to sea, and from the river unto the ends of the earth" (Psalm 72:8), that "all kings shall fall down before him" (Psalm 72:11), and that "His name shall endure for ever" (Psalm 72:17). David was well aware that he and his immediate successors did not qualify, but by faith he knew that such a king would come because of the promise of God. "He hath made with me an everlasting covenant, ordered in all things, and sure: for this is all my salvation, and all my desire..." (2 Samuel 23:5). David knew that his greater Son was his Lord and Christ (see Psalm 110:1). Daniel shared David's desire for this ideal rule, and his prophetic purpose included outlining God's faithfulness to the promise of that everlasting covenant. Every kingdom delineated by Daniel was an integral part of God's plan to inaugurate the Kingdom of His Christ. All of time progressed to its fullness when Christ came to earth the first time in great humiliation. All of time since progresses to its fullness when Christ will come again to earth in great glory. Both comings are part of that everlasting covenant, ordered in all things, and sure.

Both Nebuchadnezzar's dream of the colossus and Daniel's vision of the beasts culminate in the inevitable and everlasting kingdom of Christ. I might as well make my prophetic position clear up front. I am a premillennialist because I just can't be anything else when I read the passages in Scripture of the kingdom of Christ. This means that I believe that the Lord Jesus will return to earth personally in all of His incarnate glory and set up an earthly kingdom which He will rule personally until time transitions to eternity. Belief in an actual and physical reign of Christ on earth does not deny or contradict that Christ is now the mediatorial King who rules a spiritual kingdom. The millennial reign of Christ is a visible manifestation and administration of that mediatorial reign. As our Mediator, Christ is Prophet, Priest, and King. There was visible evidence and validation of His prophetic office at His first advent: The Word became flesh and perfectly declared God's will and way of salvation. Christ also visibly evidenced and validated His priestly office at His first advent as He offered Himself the perfect sacrifice for His people. Although the spiritual evidence of His kingly office, too, was operative during the first advent, I believe that a visible manifestation will validate it as well. I reject any notion that denies the current operation of Christ's mediatorial rule. Christ now reigns supremely as the Mediatorial King of His people, but I believe the Scripture leads us to believe in an eventual visible administration of the kingdom. What we now know by faith will one day become a matter of sight. Every eye will behold the King in His beauty, every knee will bow, and every tongue will confess that He is the King of kings. I will be assuming this premillennial orientation as we consider this new kingdom that follows the final four.

This kingdom must come, and come it will. Although these two sections of Daniel do not supply all the details of the ideal kingdom, they do highlight some important truths about the King and the nature of His kingship.

THE IDENTITY OF THE KING

A stone hewn without hands will destroy the colossus of Nebuchadnezzar's dream (2:34). One like the Son of man will come with the clouds of heaven to receive the kingdom after the destruction of the beast (7:13-14). Both of these terms–stone and Son of man–are significant: One builds on antecedent revelation; one is the foundation text for revelation to come. The stone represents Christ. The messianic consequence of the stone image goes back to Genesis. The patriarchal blessing to Joseph referred to "the mighty God of Jacob; (from thence is the shepherd, the stone of Israel)" (Genesis 49:24). Isaiah said in one of his great messianic declarations: "Therefore thus saith the Lord God, Behold, I lay in Zion for a foundation a stone, a tried stone, a precious corner stone, a sure foundation: he that believeth shall not make haste" (Isaiah 28:16). Long after Daniel, the New Testament used the same imagery with reference to Christ (Matthew 16: 13-16; 1 Peter 2:4-8). That this stone is hewn without hands makes it clear that the sending of the stone as well as its operation is divine work. If anything clearly emerges from Daniel's context, it is the Stone's absolute and irresistible power. Not even the most powerful kingdoms on earth can withstand the execution of its mission.

That Daniel sees the kingdoms of the beasts being transferred to one like the Son of man is both ironic and theologically consequential.

The irony is that God takes dominion away from beasts and gives dominion to the perfect Man. A significant parallel inheres between Daniel's vision and David's poem of the Ideal Man: "For thou hast made him a little lower than the angels, and hast crowned him with glory and honour. Thou madest him to have dominion over the works of thy hands; thou hast put all things under his feet" (Psalm 8:5-6). Dominion over all the earth and its creatures was humanity's first commission (Genesis 1:28), but man lost it through his disobedience. The day will come, however, when that dominion will be restored to the perfect Man who earned it through His obedience. The perfect Man regains everything that the first man lost. Daniel saw dominion belonging to beasts, an arrangement contrary to creation's mandate. He sees dominion returned to man, an arrangement that fulfills God's purpose. As the Curse-Reverser, Christ reverses every part of the curse; He regains all that was lost because of sin. This restoration is another reason I believe that an earthly kingdom must occur.

The theological significance of the appellation "Son of man" is that this is the first and only time the Old Testament applies the otherwise common expression to the Messiah. Daniel's use of it, although unique in the Old Testament, provides the biblical foundation for the New Testament employment of the term to refer directly to Jesus. Indeed, "Son of Man" became one of the most frequent ways Christ identified Himself. On the one hand, the expression declares humanity. The term "son" in both Hebrew and Aramaic would often designate a class of something; for instance, the idiom "sons of the prophets" does not refer to the offspring of prophets but rather to those who belonged to the class of prophets. So at least in part, "son of man" refers to one who is man. It is a fitting expression for the incarnation of the Son of God: God became man. On the other hand, although Daniel saw the coming one in terms of humanity, he also recognized the deity. Comparing 7:14 with 7:27 illustrates this link. Whereas 7:14 speaks of everlasting dominion as belonging to the Son of Man, verse 27 associates it with the Most High. The Son of Man who will descend in the clouds is indeed the God/Man. The New Testament forthrightly confirms that Jesus Christ is the One Daniel saw receiving the kingdom (Matthew 24:30; 26:64; Mark 13:26; Revelation 1:7).

THE ADMINISTRATION OF THE KING

Daniel directs most of the attention to the operation of the ideal kingdom. Four statements sum up how Daniel portrays the Kingdom of Christ. It is not my purpose to write a commentary on the text, so I will simply make each statement with brief comment.

THE KINGDOM IS ORDAINED BY GOD

"And in the days of these kings shall the God of heaven set up a kingdom" (2:44). God ordains all government (see Romans 13), including the ones that precede the establishment of Christ's. Daniel made this key point about each of the components of the colossus and each of the beasts from the sea. Not even the little horn could usurp a throne apart from God's will. Daniel's vision particularly underscores the Lord's sovereign purpose in setting up Christ's kingdom. Daniel sees the elevation of the throne of the Ancient of days (7:9). This is a title of dignity referring to God. The description of God and His throne in terms of the snowy white garments, wool-like hair, and fiery streams features His majesty, purity, glory, and justice. But the salient point for now is that the Son of Man appeared before the Ancient of days and received from Him "dominion, and glory, and a kingdom" (7:14). That Christ is Himself God means that by virtue of His eternal deity, He is absolutely sovereign: That is the essence of deity. He receives the mediatorial kingdom by virtue of His obedient Messiahship. This is the kingdom that He will in turn deliver back to the Father, according to Paul (1 Corinthians 15:24-25). If God ordained this kingdom, and Christ earned this kingdom, we can be absolutely sure that this kingdom will come.

THE KINGDOM IS UNIVERSAL

Christ's kingdom extends to the totality of the planet: Christ's kingdom is good news for everybody. This universality is unique. His will be the only one-world government in history or in prophecy. Nebuchadnezzar witnessed in his dream that the stone smashed the entire image representing gentile kingdoms and became a great mountain filling the whole earth (2:35). It is significant that the stone replaces the image. If the image represented earthly kingdoms, the only thing that can replace them is an earthly kingdom. That just makes sense, and it's another reason I'm a premillennialist. Daniel also saw that "all people, nations, and languages, should serve him" (7:14). The universality of Christ's kingdom is a frequent prophetic theme (e.g., Isaiah 2:2; Amos 9:11-12; Micah 4:1; Zechariah 8: 22). Although Daniel certainly applied the benefits of the coming kingdom to his people Israel, it is a serious and tragic mistake to limit the millennial kingdom to Israel, in terms of either geography or religion. Israel has a special place, and Jerusalem will indeed be the capital of the world. The Lord will sit on David's throne while He rules the world. And I should emphasize as well that the religion of the kingdom is not restored Judaism, but ideal Christianity–the only way men can truly serve and obey Him (7:27). I am absolutely confident that the Book of Hebrews will still be true during the millennial reign of Christ. Horatius Bonar's old hymn says it well, "No blood, no altar now, the sacrifice is o'er." If I could just add this thought: The sacrifice is forever over!

THE KINGDOM IS JUST

God's righteousness demands justice. Whereas the stone seems to smash the image to pieces for no apparent reason, stern justice terminates the reign of the fourth beast. At the throne of the Ancient of days the books were opened for judgment (7:10), and the beast was slain because of "the voice of the great words which the horn spake" (7:11). Daniel watched the execution and the disposal of the body into the burning flame (7:11). The beast got what he deserved. In a display of poetic justice, even the saints participate in some way in the judgments of the kingdom (7:18, 22, 27). According to Paul, we are supposed to know this: "Do ye not know that the saints shall judge the world?" (1 Corinthians 6:2). It is not surprising that the cross reference in my Bible directs attention to Daniel 7:22. One of Paul's faithful sayings parallels this idea as well: "If we suffer, we shall also reign with him" (2 Timothy 2:12; see also Revelation 20:6).

THE KINGDOM IS INDESTRUCTIBLE

At best, all the kingdoms of the world last a few hundred years. We have seen over and over again that kingdoms come and go. Only the kingdom of Christ is everlasting; it is indestructible. It will come, but it will never go. It may very well change the means of administration as time disappears into eternity, but it never ceases. This is a frequent point of emphasis in the texts we are considering. Daniel told Nebuchadnezzar that the stone's kingdom would "never be destroyed" and that it would "stand forever" (2:44). Here is what Daniel learned about the Son of man's kingdom: "His dominion is an everlasting dominion, which shall not pass away, and his kingdom that which shall not be destroyed" (7:14; see also 7:18, 27). There is nothing I can say to add to the clarity of the biblical statements.

If I can borrow Peter's line of reasoning, what manner of persons should we be in light of all that is certain to happen in God's program for time? The apostle encourages us according to the divine promise to "look for new heavens and a new earth, wherein dwelleth righteousness" and in that light to "be diligent that ye may be found of him in peace, without spot, and blameless" (2 Peter 3:11-14). Peter's point is simple and direct: Prophecy must bear directly on life in the here and now. The knowledge that God so orchestrates all of time to His prescribed end ought to be a source of comfort, hope, and purity. In surveying the rise and fall of the final four, we have considered some deep and glorious truths, some of which remain beyond our comprehension. Let's be sure that whether we understand it all or not, it nonetheless reaches our hearts. ❧

CHAPTER SIX

APPROACHING THE FULLNESS OF TIME: THE OPPOSITION

I am fairly undisciplined when it comes to physical exercise. I think about it a lot and often make plans to get back at it. But it doesn't take much to spoil the plans. We do have a treadmill in the basement that doubles nicely as a coat rack. Every so often I get motivated again, put on my cross-trainers, and step on the machine. To avoid the hamster-like boredom and take my mind off what I'm doing, I watch one of my hunting videos. I love to hunt, and these videos remind me in the off season why I love it and why September to January is my favorite time of the year. As I listen to successful hunters describe their experience and share advice to help me duplicate their success, I hear certain cliches over and over. "Patience pays off." "It doesn't get any better than this." "I love it when a plan comes together." I suppose we so typically express surprised delight when our plans come together because more often than not they don't. No matter what the venture hunting, exercise, business, or just daily experience–this or that factor potentially frustrates our plans. There are always unanticipated conditions that seize control and either force us into another course of action or cause us to resign ourselves to failure. Life is filled with things that happen contrary to our expectations; this is part of life under the sun. Listen to what the Preacher said:

> I returned, and saw under the sun, that the race is not to the swift, nor the battle to the strong, neither yet bread to the wise, nor yet riches to men of understanding, nor yet favour to men of skill; but time and chance happeneth to them all. For man also knoweth not his time: as the fishes that are taken in an evil net, and as the birds that are caught in the snare; so are the sons of men snared in an evil time, when it falleth suddenly upon them. (Ecclesiastes 9:11-12)

Limited knowledge of the future and of all possible concomitant circumstances drastically curtails our ability to make any certain plans at all. I, too, love it when a plan comes together.

God, however, does not see things this way. God's knowledge of all things actual and all things possible is illimitable. By nature, He is incapable of being surprised. God is not a reactionary whose next move depends on something or someone outside of Himself. As the absolute Sovereign, He is totally and uniquely independent and unaffected by external agents. As Nebuchadnezzar's confession puts it: "He doeth according to his will in the army of heaven, and among the inhabitants of the earth: and none can stay his hand" (4:35; see also Psalms 115:3 and 135:6). Consequently, God's plans are fail-proof; His plans cannot do anything else but come together. This does not mean that there is no opposition to God's plans, but rather that no opposition can stay the execution of God's plans or cause any alteration of His purpose. In fact, God is in so much control that He factors in the opposition as part of the decreed means of accomplishing His perfect will. The biblical record makes this perfectly clear.

When God first revealed His plan to reverse the curse caused by sin, He announced that it would sustain opposition. In the curse directed to the serpent-tempter, the Lord said, "I will put enmity between thee and the woman, and between thy seed and her seed; it shall bruise thy head, and thou shalt bruise his heel" (Genesis 3:15). The serpent is Satan, and the seed of the serpent refers to all who, untouched by grace, express hostility to God and affinity to Satan. The seed of the woman is the consummate enemy of Satan and the only Savior of sinners, the Lord Jesus Christ. The hostile opposition from Satan and his progeny does not threaten the success of God's plan: Christ's victory over Satan is absolutely guaranteed. The outcome is that the head of the serpent will be crushed: Crushing the head is fatal. That the serpent will bruise the heel of the woman's seed suggests the ineffectiveness of the serpent to frustrate or alter the mission of Christ: Crushing the heel is futile. From moving Herod to kill the children in hopes of murdering Jesus, to attempting to discredit Christ during the temptation, to fiercely attacking Him in the garden of Gethsemanæ on the eve of the crucifixion, Satan was constantly nipping and snapping at Christ's heels, trying to thwart the planned atonement. But he could not frustrate God's plan to reverse the curse of sin by Christ.

Genesis 3:15 is a synopsis of redemptive history; it is the Bible in a nutshell. What the first book of the Bible predicts, the last book of the Bible reiterates in overview. In apocalyptic vision, John sees the old serpent seeking to devour Christ from the moment of His birth, waging war with Michael and his angels, spewing floods against God's people, being expelled from heaven, and intensifying his wrath in light of his own certain defeat (Revelation 12). One theme runs through the vision: Every Satanic opposition fails. Satan's hostility causes the conflicts we encounter in the course of life, but his opposition does not threaten God's purposed plan. That Genesis foreshadows the conflict and Revelation bears it out confirms that even the opposition to God's plan is part of the plan. It doesn't surprise the Lord, and therefore, it shouldn't surprise us when we find ourselves engulfed in the conflict. God is in control, and we should utilize all of the armor and armaments that He has provided for our protection so that we "may be able to stand against the wiles of devil" and "be able to quench all the fiery darts of the wicked" (Ephesians 6:11, 16).

Letting us know about the opposition up front is a way for the Lord to encourage us to faith and confidence when the opposition comes. I think, for instance, that this partly explains why God told Moses beforehand that He would harden Pharaoh's heart, leaving the divinely manipulated king in turn to harden his own heart and refuse to let the people go. Although the Bible does not report it, I can almost hear Moses saying the first time Pharaoh rejected his request, "Yes! I love it when a plan comes together." Pharaoh's opposition was a built-in contributor to the achieving of God's glory, the ultimate aim of all God's plans (Exodus 14:4, 17). Daniel learned firsthand about spiritual warfare when in a vision he discovered that the answer to his prayers was postponed for three weeks due to a real but unseen battle between "the prince of the kingdom of Persia" and the pre-incarnate Christ allied with "Michael, one of the chief princes" (10:13). My inability to fathom this kind of spiritual contest has no bearing on its reality. But notwithstanding the opposition, Daniel's prayer was answered, and the Lord revealed the certain events that would work together to the prescribed end (10:14). The "scripture of truth" (10:21) could not be broken. Recognition that opposition is an integral element in God's plan is a vital tenet in a biblically sound theology of time. So rather than sinking in despair when we encounter opposition, we should echo my imagined words of Moses, "Yes! I love it when a plan comes together."

Daniel develops this element of time theology in a most remarkable way. Concentrating on Nebuchadnezzar's dream (chapter 2) and the first of Daniel's several visions (chapter 7), we have already seen the big picture–the rise and fall of the final four. The big picture was unquestionably the operation of God's sovereign will. In the visions recorded in Daniel 8 (near the end of the Babylonian regime) and 11 (at the beginning of the Persian regime), the macroscopic view becomes microscopic. It is unquestionably certain that all the specific details are the operation of God's sovereign will as well. God leaves nothing to chance; nothing just happens. In these two visions, attention focuses on the development of the kingdoms of Medo-Persia and Greece. From Daniel's perspective these were the two principal kingdoms standing between him and the fullness of time when Christ would first come. Then with a typical prophetic time-jump Daniel leaps to the kingdom of the future Antichrist. From our perspective his is the principal kingdom standing between us and the second fullness of time when Christ will come again. The theme of opposition is quite obvious as Daniel previews the events approaching the fullness of times. But we must keep in mind that the very fact that God reveals the opposition beforehand is evidence that He is in control of the whole operation. His will is being done; His kingdom is coming. Nothing can stop it.

OPPOSITION TO THE FIRST FULLNESS OF TIME

The Aramaic section of Daniel starts and finishes with the overview of the final four gentile kingdoms. Interestingly, when Daniel puts the spotlight on the opposition factor, he shifts from writing in Aramaic to Hebrew. Aramaic, the international language, was the appropriate vehicle for conveying the message of the big picture as it relates to the history of the world in general. Hebrew, the native language of Israel, was the appropriate vehicle for conveying the relevance of the details of that big picture to God's people specifically. Most of what Daniel saw in the visions of chapters 8 and 11 transpired in the Intertestamental Period, the approximately four hundred years between the close of the Old Testament canon and the beginning of the New Testament revelation. This itself suggests an important truth. Although these were years of divine silence, they were not years of divine inactivity. Revelation temporarily ceased, but redemptive history progressed on schedule according to plan. This design, by the way, is just as true for us. Revelation ceased with the close of the New Testament canon, but redemptive history is progressing on schedule according to God's plan and will culminate in all that divine revelation said it would. These may be days of divine silence, but they are not days of divine inactivity.

As we consider the part of Daniel's vision that predicted the events of the Intertestamental Period, we once again have an advantage over Daniel himself since these events are now history. We can add the names, dates, and places. In doing so, we will have to be impressed with how precise the prophecies were. In fact, these are the visions that particularly cause unbelieving critics so much consternation. The details are so precise that the critic–minus a belief in supernatural inspiration–feels constrained to relegate the prophecies to a time period after the events: They must be history, or at the least, eyewitness records. Belief in supernatural inspiration, however, eliminates any surprise about the accuracy. It is because God knows and orchestrates time that He is able to communicate it beforehand to His prophets. To illustrate, I want to look first at the facts of the prophecy and then the facts of history.

THE FACTS OF THE VISION

In his second vision Daniel was transported to the river of Ulai in the province of Elam, just north of the Persian Gulf (8:1-2). As so often happens to the recipients of divine revelations via visions, Daniel was an active participant in the process. Although Daniel remained bodily in Babylon, he saw himself by a river's bank in Persian territory witnessing more strange symbols involving odd animal shapes and behavior. To his and our advantage, this time Gabriel appeared to connect the visionary symbols to their referents in the real world. So as I rehearse the facts of what Daniel saw, I might as well use Gabriel's clues that focus attention on three principal objects.

The first thing Daniel saw was a two-horned ram whose horns were uneven–one was higher than the other but the more elevated one was not always the higher of the two (8:3). As Daniel watched, the ram was charging in every direction except eastward, and nothing could stop its progress. It had free course to go where it wanted, and it became great in the process (8:4). Gabriel informed Daniel, "The ram which thou sawest having two horns are the kings of Media and Persia" (8:20). Thanks to Gabriel, this one is easy.

The second thing Daniel saw was a billy goat with a conspicuous horn between its eyes that was moving so fast its feet never touched the ground (8:5). With fury and speed, the goat butted the ram, breaking its two horns and stomping it into the ground (8:6-7). After the billy goat had marked and claimed his turf, the conspicuous horn was broken and replaced by four others, each pointing in a different direction (8:8). Notwithstanding the oddities of the goat, again–thanks to Gabriel–there is no question concerning its identity: "And the rough goat is the king of Grecia: and the great horn that is between his eyes is the first king" (8:22). The angelic interpreter goes on to identify the four replacement horns as four kingdoms that collectively will rule the goat's domain but that individually lack the power of the first king.

The third thing Daniel saw was a little horn that grew out of one of the four horns of the billy goat (8:9). The actions of this little horn constitute the primary point of interest and relate most directly to our theme of opposition. Daniel watched as the power of this little horn increased toward the south (a reference to Egypt), east (a reference to Mesopotamia and beyond), and the pleasant land (most likely a reference to Palestine according to Jeremiah 3:19). Much of the little horn's furor was directed against heaven itself with apparent success as both the stars (a likely reference to God's people) and truth were cast to the ground and trampled (8:10-12). Gabriel doesn't name any names, but he does make it terribly clear that a fierce king would arise whose power would not be his own but who would be vehement in his opposition to the holy people (8:24) and even against "the Prince of princes" (8:25). Thankfully, Gabriel adds a piece of information about the little horn that Daniel didn't see in the vision: "He shall be broken without hand" (8:25). God Himself will take him down; no opposition can prevail against the Lord and His plan. This is the truth to keep constantly before us.

THE FACTS OF HISTORY

Such are the details of Daniel's vision that about the only information history adds is specific names, dates, and places. Because the Medo-

Persian Empire, the two-horned ram of this vision, corresponds to the chest and arms of Nebuchadnezzar's dream and the lopsided bear of Daniel's first vision, I do not need to repeat the historical facts we considered in our discussion of the final four. It is worthy to note once again, however, how precisely the particulars of the symbolic beast match what became reality. The staggered horns, the tallest of which gained the priority, depict the prominence of Persia over Media that was due primarily to Cyrus.

Picturing Greece perfectly, the fast-moving, angry, one-horned billy goat that developed four horns parallels the torso and thighs of the colossus in Daniel 2 and the four-headed, four-winged leopard of the unnatural menagerie in Daniel 7. Historical records are replete with evidence of Alexander's speedy triumphs and the particular rancor he harbored against the Persians for their atrocities committed against Greek cities, particularly during the administration of Xerxes. That spirit of revenge most likely accounts for Alexander's execution of the male citizens of Persepolis, the Persian capital, and the burning of Xerxes's palace in spite of the city's attempt to surrender. Although Nebuchadnezzar's dream represented sufficiently well the basic facts about Greece, both of Daniel's visions particularly highlight the swiftness and vengeance of Alexander's conquests followed in turn by the division of his realm into four parts under the management of Antipater, Lysimachus, Ptolemy, and Seleucus, his generals. Again, I have already surveyed the salient historical facts of this period in the chapter on the final four. This second vision of Daniel, however, goes beyond the mere division of the Greek Empire and zeroes in on the one part that bears directly on God's people: the opposition to the fullness of time.

Although Gabriel's interpretation does not specifically identify which of the four parts is in the prophetic focus, his explanation offers those of us on this side of the fulfillment enough to name names. Fulfilled prophecy is always clear, and it is undoubtedly clear that Daniel's vision isolates the Seleucid quarter of the empire generally and the rule of Antiochus Epiphanes specifically. Antiochus IV, or Epiphanes (i.e., manifest), is the little horn. Daniel 11:1-35 contains an astonishingly minute prophecy of the development of the Seleucid dynasty leading to Antiochus IV and his reign of terror (175-164 B.C.). So precise is it that I will take you through verse by verse and fulfillment by fulfillment in appendix 3. For now, I will just provide an overview as it relates directly to Daniel's vision and Gabriel's interpretation in Daniel 8.

Although Antiochus IV is the primary antagonist in view, he actually marked the culmination of an evolving conflict between the Seleucids and Ptolemies that caught the Jews in the middle. The initial distribution of Alexander's kingdom allotted the territory of Syria eastward to India to Seleucus and the territory south of Syria including Palestine and Egypt to Ptolemy. Palestine's position as the land bridge linking Syria and Egypt, the two principal seats of power, made it vulnerable whenever the two rivals plotted or moved against each other. By the time Antiochus IV shrewdly and treacherously assumed power, tensions were high between the two divisions of the Greek Empire, and to complicate matters the increasing influence of Rome affected the balance of power. I've included further information about all that in the appendix.

Both Daniel and Gabriel focus specifically on the actions of the little horn against the pleasant land. The horn violates the sanctuary, interferes with the worship system, slaughters many of the saints, and defies the Lord Himself (8:10-12, 24-25). Although many factors contributed to his display of cruelty against the Jews, at the heart of it was his fundamental policy of unifying the heterogeneous population he ruled by inculcating Greek culture into every society. Antiochus regarded himself as a manifestation of Zeus–hence his nickname "Epiphanes"–and Hellenization was the missionary glue for cultural unity. If I can speak anachronistically, this was the proverbial time bomb that was certain to explode in Israel. If the exile cured the Jews of anything, it was their pre-exilic propensity to polytheism. Orthodox monotheism and Greek polytheism were glaringly incompatible.

History records that Antiochus did in fact meddle in Jewish affairs and on multiple occasions perpetrated violence against both the people and their religion. Here are a few examples. During his reign, Onias III, the legitimate high priest was assassinated, and Jason, a usurper of the post, was placed in the office with the understanding that he would help implement Antiochus's policies. A gymnasium was constructed for games. Given our understanding of sport and exercise, that might seem to us a benign gesture of good will. Sports were as fun then as they are now and plainly alluring to the young men. But since the Greek games were associated with the cult of Hercules and involved nudity and the consequent exposure of circumcision, participation resulted in religious compromise and, even worse, in apostasy, according to conservative Jews. Antiochus's encroachments into Jewish life intensified from temptation to forced compliance and outright violence. On one occasion on his return from Egypt, Antiochus attacked Jerusalem, plundered the temple and removed sacred vessels and furniture, slaughtered thousands of Jews, and enslaved others.

Eventually, he took over the city and overturned Jewish customs and religious practices. He suspended the temple sacrifices and Sabbath observances. He destroyed copies of the Law and outlawed circumcision. He forced the eating of pork upon the penalty of death. He erected shrines to Greek gods throughout the land and, in an ultimate act of contempt, desecrated the temple by making it a shrine to Zeus and offering swine on the altar. This act most likely is that "abomination that maketh desolate" (11:31). Antiochus did what he could–whether out of rage, spite, or his own religious convictions–to eradicate God's chosen people and their distinctiveness in the world.

Opposition is almost too feeble a word to describe the blatant disregard for what was in that dispensation the scripturally proper way to worship the one true and living God. Had Antiochus succeeded in his tyrannical oppression, he would have indeed hindered the progress of time to its messianic fullness. Old Testament prophecies and New Testament declarations make it clear that certain things had to be in place when Messiah came, and Antiochus threatened their existence. For instance, Malachi had predicted that the Christ would appear suddenly in the temple (Malachi 3:1). I state the obvious, but that means that there had to be a temple in place. If Christ were to fulfill all the demands of the law, there had to be a religious mechanism in place for that to happen. For example, it was written in the law, "Every male that openeth the womb shall be called holy to the Lord" (Luke 2:23; cf. Exodus 13:2). It was then necessary "to offer a sacrifice according to that which is said in the law of the Lord" (Luke 2: 24; cf. Leviticus 12:8). Had there been no temple and no people dedicated to the strict observance of Old Testament law, the parents of Jesus would not have been able to do for Jesus "after the custom of the law" (Luke

2:27). The wonderful fact is that a temple was in place and a religious mechanism was operating all according to plan. In fact, God used the opposition of Antiochus to guarantee that those things would be in place. When the Lord was finished with Antiochus, He brought him to a reportedly painful death in semi-exile after frustrating setbacks in his plans to Hellenize and to plunder other parts of his kingdom. He was "broken without hand" (8:25). Antiochus is a casebook study in God's using the wrath of men to procure praise to Himself (Psalm 76:10). God's purpose always prevails.

I need to digress a little here in order to stress the import of Antiochus's reign of terror on New Testament history. Many of the Jewish customs and institutions that were operating when Christ came originated in this crucial period between the Testaments. Broadly speaking, three Jewish groups emerged in reaction to Antiochus: the Maccabbeans (military resisters), the Hellenists (political compromisers), and the Hasidim (religious separatists). These groups sum up the prophecy: "And such as do wickedly against the covenant shall he corrupt by flatteries: but the people that do know their God shall be strong, and do exploits" (11:32). The Hellenists and the offspring of the Hasidim remained into New Testament times. Of all the movements developing from this period, the Hasidim (pious ones) were primarily responsible for preserving the religious system necessary for the coming of Christ. Unhappily, the movement that was so faithful in preparing the way for Christ became one of the greatest instruments of opposition when He came. In all likelihood, the Hasidim were the predecessors of the Pharisees (separated ones), the religious order that was most vehemently aggressive in its opposition to Jesus Christ.

There is a terrible irony in that opposition that stands as a sobering warning. In their protest of the pagan encroachments of

Antiochus, the Hasidim maintained strict adherence to the law of God and devised safeguards for its protection. In their effort to preserve the sanctity of the law, they specified applications of obedience designed to address the particular pressures of the day. Their motives were good and pure, and I believe that many of them were true believers, waiting and looking "for redemption in Jerusalem" (Luke 2:38). They were the fundamentalists of the day. Tragically, it wasn't long before the traditions of their applications gained equal status and identification with the law itself. What they sought to protect became redefined and perverted in the process. They erected a fence around the law that eventually became the law itself in their thinking. So convinced were they of their religious correctness that they accused the perfectly righteous Son of God of breaking the law. It is true enough that Christ often violated the Pharisaical traditions and transgressed their fence, but the truth of the matter is that in order to keep perfectly the law of God, He had to break the laws of the Pharisees. In their legalistic pride and hypocrisy, it never crossed their minds that they could be wrong.

Herein lies the potential danger inherent in some segments of modern fundamentalism. Too often in the rush to scriptural relevancy and Christian practicality, applications of principles are made without due and necessary attention to what the Bible itself says. What to do takes precedence over why something should be done. Such dogmatism about particular applications of the Scripture can result that, just as was true with the Pharisees, practice assumes parity with Bible itself. Those who don't conform precisely and minutely to the outlined standards for conduct suffer the accusation of being compromisers or worse. I wonder sometimes if the Lord Himself would be accepted in some spheres of fundamentalism. Please don't misunderstand what I am saying. I am speaking as a fundamentalist myself–at least in terms of the historic use of that word. I sincerely believe that the Bible is the only rule for faith and practice. Indeed, if what we believe doesn't translate into practice, it really doesn't constitute belief. Christianity is more than just creedal theory; it is a way of life flowing from both a personal relationship with Christ and the propositional truths of God's Word. But we must be willing to see the difference between the authority of the Bible and our preferences concerning practices, regardless of how convinced we are of our own rightness. It may very well be that others who believe the Bible with the same degree of fervency can with the same intensity of conviction have different and equally legitimate preferences in application. I am speaking, of course, regarding those spheres of life where the Scripture allows the liberty of conscience, and not in the clearly black-and-white issues of obedience or disobedience. There are definitely clear-cut areas of right and wrong–whether some Christians acknowledge them or not. This digression is going far beyond my outline for this chapter, but we must learn from history. The drift of the Hasidim to the Pharisees raises a red flag. Let us heed the warning lest our religion stand in opposition to Christ. The sad thing is that it can happen.

Back to the point. When Antiochus vented his rage against the Jews and their whole system of religious life, from a human perspective the progress of redemptive history seemed to be in serious jeopardy. But spiritually speaking, appearance and reality are seldom the same. God used the intense opposition to solidify the circumstances that Scripture required for the coming of Christ. When the opposition served its divinely intended purpose, God recompensed the evil for evil. The promise was never in jeopardy after all. And "when the fulness of time was come, God sent forth his Son, made of a woman, made under the law" (Galatians 4:4). The eternal plan came together.

OPPOSITION TO THE SECOND FULLNESS OF TIME

It was God's plan to send His Son the first time to be offered as a sacrifice "to bear the sins of many" (Hebrews 9:28). It is God's plan that Christ will "appear the second time without sin unto salvation" (Hebrews 9:28). The precise timing of the second appearing is a divine secret (Matthew 24:36; Acts 1:7), but there is a set time whose fullness will come. Just as certainly as Christ had to come and did come the first time, He has to come and will come the second time. The opposition of the serpent and its seed against the first coming did not prevent it; indeed, God factored the opposition into the plan and used it to accomplish His purpose. In the face of all the wicked conspiracies against the Lord and His Christ, the Sovereign Lord sat in heaven laughing and holding the conspirators in derision (Psalm 2:2, 4). It is no different regarding the Second Coming of Christ. As the day approaches, Heaven still echoes with divine laughter over the folly of all the futile plans of earth and hell to rebel against the Lord and His Christ. The opposition to the completion of redemptive history will be intense–indeed, more intense than ever before in the history of the world. The devil's wrath steadily increases and will boil over as the end nears "because he knoweth that he hath but a short time" (Revelation 12:12). Although his head was fatally wounded by Christ on the cross and he suffers defeat with every advance of the church (Romans 16:20), the devil goes around like a roaring lion "seeking whom he may devour" (1 Peter 5:8). An enemy never appears to be more dangerous than when he knows his days are numbered and his cause is hopeless. Notwithstanding the swelling severity of hostilities against God, Christ, and the church as time approaches its end, we need not worry, because God has included the opposition in the script of His plan. This inclusion rests on more than divine prescience; it represents an integral part of the divine decree.

Again, one of the evidences that opposition is part of God's plan is the fact that the Bible predicts it. Such prophetic predictions are possible because God created, owns, and uses time according to His prerogative. I have emphasized that the enmity between the seed of the serpent and the Seed of the woman that started in Eden has been and remains a constant in the course of redemptive history. It is to be expected that the heat of the enmity should climax at the critical moments in the execution of God's redemptive purpose. Although opposition to the church collectively and Christians individually has always existed, I believe that standing between us and the Second Coming of Christ is a satanically inspired assault against God the like of which the world has never seen. Listen to what the Lord Jesus Himself said about this. "For then shall be great tribulation, such as was not since the beginning of the world to this time, no, nor ever shall be. And except those days should be shortened, there should no flesh be saved: but for the elect's sake those days shall be shortened" (Matthew 24:21-22). It is the coming of the Son of man "in the clouds of heaven with power and great glory" that shortens those days (Matthew 24:30; note the use of Daniel's language from 7:13). The presence of trouble is evidence that God's plan is coming together.

Not only does Daniel make remarkable predictions about events leading up to Christ's first coming, but he jumps ahead in his visions to events immediately preceding the Second Coming as well. His focus on these two great epochs does not deny God's control of intervening times, but rather establishes the truth of it. That is the logic of prophecy in regard to a theology of time. God's control of the future attests to His control of the present. I am more concerned about our learning this lesson for our theology of time than simply charting out what we can about the end times, as interesting as that may be. Therefore, as we consider a little about how Daniel describes the consummate enemy of God who will engender terrible tribulation in the world and then meet his unhappy end, we should take heart in the lesser tribulations that we confront in our times. We should not be shaken by them, because Christ let us know up front that they are part of the plan: "In the world ye shall have tribulation: but be of good cheer; I have overcome the world" (John 16:33). As it was during the Intertestamental tribulation and as it will certainly be during the eschatological tribulation, so must it be in our day that "the people that do know their God shall be strong, and do exploits" (11:32).

I am keenly aware of the many differing interpretations regarding the aspects of Daniel's prophecy that are yet unfulfilled. That's the nature of prophecy. We could conduct an exhaustive search of commentaries and still not find any two that agree tit for tat with every constituent part of Daniel's visions. Until the prophecies are fulfilled, the details and mechanics of fulfillment may remain cryptic. If we keep in mind that my objective is not to defend any eschatological program but to instill within our hearts a reassuring confidence in God's sovereignty, then even those who may disagree with my eschatological presuppositions and particular analyses can benefit from this book. Having issued this caveat, let me state that I believe Daniel's visions reveal a future Antichrist, alias the man of sin, the son of perdition (2 Thessalonians 2:3), and the beast (Revelation 13:1). Based on the data of both Daniel and Revelation, I believe that his reign of terror will occur during a seven-year period of tribulation–what Jeremiah calls "the time of Jacob's trouble" (30:7) and what Daniel dates to the 70th week (9:27)–that will end with Christ's glorious return. Since according to my presuppositions there is not yet any history to review, all I can do is outline the facts of Daniel's vision. But I should say a word first about the mechanics of the vision.

In the visions of chapters 8 and 11, Daniel employs two prophetic techniques to introduce the man of sin who will lead the opposition against the Lord in the end times. First, he uses Antiochus Epiphanes, the Intertestamental opponent, as a picture prophecy of the Antichrist, the eschatological opponent. This portrayal illustrates the relationship between type and antitype. It builds on points of similarity between the historical figure (the type) and the future figure (the antitype). What Antiochus would do and now has done is in some significant ways analogous to what the future Antichrist will do. The very use of Antiochus as a divinely appointed illustration of his future counterpart evinces God's ultimate control of the whole scene. God can use something in history to point to something in the future for the simple reason that He governs both. The hermeneutical temptation in reading types is to multiply the points of analogy. Yielding to that temptation usually results in numerous parallels of doubtful merit rather than just those points intended. Learn to look for the main lesson. At the very least, Antiochus points to the certain doom of every enemy of God, regardless of how powerful he assumes himself to be.

Second, Daniel uses the technique of progressive prediction, sometimes called prophetic telescoping. In other words, in the same prophetic discourse, he leaps from one prophecy to another without noting or regarding gaps of time between them. This is the device employed, for instance, in Daniel's prophecy of the Seventy Weeks (9: 24-27). I believe (along with many others) that after a predictive unit focusing on events associated with the first sixty-nine weeks, Daniel presents an indeterminate temporal gap before the commencement of the seventieth week, which reveals important facts about the Antichrist. Particularly in the vision of chapter 11, Daniel skips from Intertestamental opposition to eschatological opposition without warning or clue. Knowing what we do about how the prophecies of Antiochus were fulfilled, we almost immediately apprehend that Antiochus is no longer in view. But even those who agree with my basic analysis don't always agree exactly where the shift takes place. I confess that I'm not altogether sure where it does, either, but I am sure it does. I think Daniel 11 reveals three key truths about the coming Antichrist. Since I am making no claims to write a commentary, I will just highlight those truths and include a couple of thoughts from Daniel 9 as well.

First, he will be anti-God. The text is explicitly clear: "And the king shall do according to his will; and he shall exalt himself, and magnify himself above every god" (11:36). His atheism is consistent and complete. He will blaspheme the God of gods (11:36). "God of gods" is a Hebrew idiom designating a superlative: it refers to the supreme God, the one true and living God. The blasphemy of this anti-God king will be extraordinary, as he will speak dreadful and unheard of things (cf. 7:25). His atheism extends to a disregard for the "God of his fathers" (11:37). Since the Authorized Version has capitalized

"God," some interpreters have gone so far as to say the coming Antichrist must be a Jew. The expression could be translated literally as "gods of his fathers." I prefer this rendition. The reference is not, then, to the true God, but to ancestral deities. The Antichrist may be willing to use religion to advance his own cause, but he worships no god other than himself: "He shall magnify himself above all" (11:37). This, by the way, is one reason that I do not think Antiochus IV is any longer in the picture. Remember that much of what the Seleucid king did was motivated by his devotion to Greek culture which was inseparably linked to Greek religion. Most significant is the fact that the future Antichrist has no regard for "the desire of women." This earns him the epithet "Antichrist." I suggest that this expression "the desire of women" directly refers to Christ, the promised virgin-born Seed of the woman. It may well indicate the hope of every believing woman in Daniel's day that she might be that woman chosen to bear the Messiah. Obviously, those living at the time of Christ's Second Coming will know who the mother of Christ was, but it is a fitting expression for those in Daniel's day who lived before Christ's first coming. Implementing the Analogy of Faith rule of interpretation makes it clear that Daniel and Paul are describing the same person. Paul identified the man of sin as he "Who opposeth and exalteth himself above all that is called God, or that is worshipped; so that he as God sitteth in the temple of God, shewing himself that he is God" (2 Thessalonians 2:4).

Second, he will be obsessed with power. Although he rejects all gods, verse 38 says that he will honor "the God of forces," literally, a god of fortresses. Rather than naming a personal deity, this phrase refers to the power of his military machine to which he will direct all his resources and which he will use ruthlessly to advance his kingdom. Although his power will be extensive, it will not be universal. He will meet resistance from the kings of the north and south who will advance against him with able armies of their own (11:40). I have no idea who those kings will be specifically, and those who have ideas are only guessing. Whoever they are, they will have only limited success against him. Some nations will escape his control (11:41); he will subdue others (11:42-43). Interestingly and significantly, the northern and southern coalition will divert his attention to "the glorious land," a reference to Israel (11:41). Daniel 9 especially emphasizes the relationship of a coming prince and the inhabitants of Israel (9:26). The prince ultimately destroys the city and the sanctuary but only after breaking what appears to be peace treaty with Israel that he brokered at the beginning of the seventieth week, the seven-year tribulation period (9:27). For a while the Middle East will experience that elusive peace. Something happens, however, after three and a half years, during the middle of that prophetic week (cf. the "time and times and the dividing of time" in 7:25), to cause a change in his policy toward Israel that results in the abominable desolation. My guess is that the north/south alliance of 11:40 precipitates the breaking of the covenant and motivates the atrocities in Jerusalem. Controlling Palestine will be essential to his defense against the coalition. Just like Antiochus, his ancient type, he will establish a stronghold in that region covering most of Palestine and Egypt and thereby increase his wealth significantly (11:43). Happily, his ascendancy will be only temporary.

Third, he will be doomed. Not long after he gains control over Palestine, a report of more trouble from the east and north infuriates him, and he takes off on a rampage to destroy and to devote to destruction as many as he can (11:44). Using Jerusalem as his headquarters for his last stand, he meets his end with none coming to his rescue (11:45). Daniel 9 declares tersely but marvelously that the decreed end will come upon the one who makes desolate (9:27). Daniel does not disclose what that decreed end will be, but John does. When the "KING OF KINGS, AND LORD OF LORDS" appears, he will take the beast, the Antichrist, along with his chief advisor, the false prophet, and cast them "alive into a lake of fire burning with brimstone"(Revelation 19:16, 20). That is a fearfully just ending for this consummate enemy of God and a happy ending for God's people.

The accomplished destruction of the Antichrist along with his anti-God, anti-truth system will be cause for heavenly praise: "Alleluia; Salvation, and glory, and honour, and power, unto the Lord our God: For true and righteous are his judgments" (Revelation 19: 1b-2a). The certainty of Antichrist's failure and destruction ought to be reason for Christians to praise the Lord now and live in this world with bold confidence, knowing that when the future opposition comes, it comes according to God's plan. I hope that the attention we have given in this chapter to details of history and shadows of prophecy has not distracted from the primary lesson I want to extract from the past and future. Since God is immutable, what was true in the past and what will be true in the future is true in the present. Opposition does not mean that God's purpose has been jeopardized or has veered off its best and eternally fixed course. God is in such tight of control of time and circumstance that He factors in opposition as part of the means of achieving His end. The opposition never threatens Him, and it is designed to work always for our good (Romans 8:28). Let's employ one of the apostle Paul's favorite principles of logic: reasoning from the greater to the lesser. If the Lord controls the two most intense demonstrations of humanistic and hellish opposition to His eternal purpose in Christ, then certainly He controls and uses for His glory and our good all the particular problems along the way. Contrary to what the blasphemous heresy of open theism propounds, God is not waiting to see what the creature will do so that He can calculate His next move. On the contrary, He sits on the throne of His sovereignty with no slack in the reins of His rule. So the next time we encounter trouble or opposition at any level–personally or corporately–let us have the faith to know that the trouble or opposition is certain evidence that God's plan is coming together. Everything is on course. Trusting the Lord in the bad times as well as the good times is a crucial application of a biblically based theology of time. ⊰⊱

CHAPTER SEVEN

APPROACHING THE FULLNESS OF TIME: THE CHRIST

A ll of time and, for that matter, all of eternity converge on Christ. His first coming marks the center of time; His Second Coming marks the climax. By center, I do not imply the mathematical middle of moments from creation to consummation. That would invite all kinds of crackpot calculations concerning both the date of creation and the date of the Lord's return. Many–and, for some reason particularly radio preachers–suffer the embarrassment of such miscalculations and thereby warn us of the folly of playing that game. Only the Lord knows the precise moment of both time's beginning and its end. By center, then, I mean that the Incarnation was the pivotal point to which all of Pre-Incarnation history inexorably moved and from which all of Incarnation history purposefully proceeds. Daniel's time was approaching the pivotal point; our time approaches the climax when Christ returns to commence a new era that transitions to eternity. Just as certainly as Daniel's time arrived at the center, so will ours reach the culmination point. Time is God's servant, and it obeys His will. Time is the kingdom of God's providence in which He governs all things to His eternally designated end.

Before going any further, I want to make sure that we are not entertaining any vague or incorrect conceptions about divine providence. I asked a seminary student one time to define providence. After the predictable student silence, he fumbled the response, "It's kind of like fatalism." After I labeled him a pagan and facetiously threatened to bring out the matches reserved for those making such unorthodox statements, I emphasized the important difference between divine providence and the fatalistic notion that whatever will be will be. A belief in providence understands that God has decreed the end from the beginning as well as all of the necessary in-between things that contribute to and ultimately accomplish the intended end. It operates according to the divine wisdom that knows the best possible way to achieve the best possible end. Nothing happens by chance; everything happens according to God's wisdom. Here is a key component in the proper understanding of providence: Belief in the end that God has decreed requires our belief in and diligent use of the means that God has decreed to achieve that end. That is, proper belief in providence never breeds inactivity or fateful resignation but rather obedient and expectant activity. For instance, there ought to be no more fervent evangelist than one who believes in God's eternal decree of election. Since the elect must exercise faith and faith comes by hearing the Word of God and hearing the Word of God requires the preaching of it (see Paul's logic in Romans 10), believing in election necessarily generates evangelism. Only a perverted view of election fosters passivity. So it is in every sphere of providence. We must use the means that God has commanded to accomplish the end that God has ordained. I am saying all this because the section in Daniel addressing the approach of the fullness of time when Christ comes is a classic example of merging the means and the end.

It is not surprising that Daniel, who reveals so much about God's orchestration of time, records a vision that details a series of significant events which lead to the two principal epochs of God's purpose regarding Christ: His first and Second Coming. Daniel 9 gives insight into that last stretch of time leading to the divinely determined fullness and beyond. The vision of the Seventy Weeks, one of the best-known and most controversial of all of Daniel's prophecies, is a model of prophetic telescoping that previews epochal events separated by some indeterminate amount of time. The famous prophetic vision illustrates some of the inherent ambiguities of prophetic chronology. Even though the passage is focusing on time periods, some uncertainty inheres concerning the nature of the temporal symbolism (weeks) and the exact circumstance that marks the beginning of the reckoning. Nonetheless, that Messiah is the primary focus stands without question. This, by the way, is one of the few Old Testament texts that actually uses the word "Messiah" to designate the coming Redeemer.

Whatever may be unclear about the Seventy Weeks, it is clear, as always, that Christ is the answer to every problem. He is the answer for time and eternity. Volumes have been written concerning these seventy weeks, and many writers attempt to squeeze into the weeks or between them notions completely foreign to Daniel's context or argument. It is not my purpose to address or attempt to correct what I regard as erroneous notions about this prophecy. I do, however, want to discuss briefly some of the key points and interpretation issues that should help us see how marvelously this text pinpoints the fact and the time of Christ's coming to be the Redeemer. God had promised a Savior for sinners, and nothing would or could hinder that promise, for all the promises of God are yea and amen in Christ (2 Corinthians 1:20).

It is not without significance that this certain promise concerning the coming of Christ follows one of the most outstanding prayers recorded in Scripture. Prayer is one of the God-ordered means to achieve His ordered purpose. It will do us good to consider both the means and the end. A proper theology of time excludes fatalism and requires the believing utilization of every means of grace God has given us.

THE MEANS TO THE END

Daniel 9 illustrates two general lessons: one about prayer (the means) and one about Christ (the end). The lesson about Christ is one we have seen again and again: God's purpose in Christ is certain regardless of appearances to the contrary. As Daniel prayed, the chosen nation had recently passed from subjugation to one foreign power, the Babylonians, to another, the Persians. No king occupied David's throne; it appeared impossible for God to keep His promise of the Seed of David. This period of the seventy divinely decreed weeks was God's "not to worry" to Daniel. The promised Seed of Woman progressed to the Seed of Abraham and then to the Seed of David. In no way could He fail to appear in the fullness of time. So the apparent roadblock to the coming of Christ was not reason for despair; it was reason for prayer, and this passage teaches us about the power of prayer. Daniel on his knees was mightier than any power on any earthly throne. Daniel's prayer testifies to the absolute sovereignty of God that makes praying a sensible, reasonable act of faith. If God were not ruling from His throne, prayer would be a vain act. A belief in God's absolute sovereignty does not stifle prayer; it legitimizes it. Because this is one of the model prayers in the Bible, I want to reflect on some of its specific lessons. Since I have delimited myself from writing a commentary, I will only outline the pattern of prayer that we should learn to imitate and implement in our personal use of this means of grace.

PRAYER FLOWS FROM THE WORD OF GOD

Daniel's prayer shows the vital link between God's Word and prayer, both of which are means of grace; it teaches how to use God's Word as the basis for prayer. Daniel had read in Jeremiah that the Babylonian captivity would last for seventy years (Daniel 9: 2; cf. Jeremiah 25:11; 29:10). Calculating how long he had been in Babylon, Daniel claimed that promise and began pleading with God to fulfill His Word. Knowing God's will gave him confidence and expectation in his prayer. Daniel's praying did not change the date of the divinely prescribed end to the captivity, but Daniel's praying did express his desire and eager expectancy for God's will to be done. Knowing the will of God did not make prayer needless; it made it necessary. Praying for God's will to be done guarantees the answer to prayer and expresses the necessary sense of dependence on the Lord. The fulfillment of God's promise is not a matter of "if"; it is matter of "when." If God has purposed and promised to bless His people, then we can plead with confidence and expectation that He will bless us. God's Word should both fuel our faith and define our petitions. God must keep His Word. Christ taught us to pray by precept what Daniel taught us by example: "Thy kingdom come. Thy will be done in earth, as it is in heaven" (Matthew 6:10). If we learn to pray according to this pattern, we will soon learn that God never says "No" to His will. Prayer is a means of conforming our wills to His, and that is good. The more we know His word, the more we can effectively pray.

PRAYER FOCUSES ON THE PERSON OF GOD

Prayer is a vehicle of worship, and God is the sole object of worship. Throughout this model prayer, Daniel fastens his gaze on the Lord, meditates on the Divine perfections, and thus fuels his faith even more. This orientation is clear from the start: "And I set my face unto the Lord God...And I prayed unto the LORD my God, and made my confession, and said, O Lord, the great and dreadful God, keeping the covenant and mercy to them that love him, and to them that keep his commandments..." (Daniel 9:3-4). The way Daniel addresses the Lord at the beginning and throughout the prayer highlights four essential truths about the Lord that deserve remembering as we pray.

First, the Lord is majestic. The person of God is awe-inspiring: He is worthy of fear and worship. That Daniel so frequently uses the title "Lord" (Adonai) reveals his consciousness that he is entering the presence of the sovereign King. The many references to "God" (either Elohim or El), which occur in all but five verses of the prayer, testify to his knowledge of the Lord's transcendence and creative power. This repetition is not vain nor does it represent thoughtless verbal pausing. It is part of his argument as he is praying to One who has the power and authority to do what he asks.

Second, the Lord is faithful. Verse four makes this point expressly: "keeping the covenant and mercy to them that love him." God is always loyal to His word and to His people. The Psalmist declared and Daniel relied on the unchanging truth that the covenant mercy or loyalty of the Lord endures forever (see Psalm 136). God's promises are sure, and that is good reason to pray. That Daniel also addresses the Lord as "LORD" reveals his awareness of the covenant relationship that he enjoyed with God. This capitalized spelling in the Authorized

Version, of course, designates the unique name of God, Jehovah. This personal name reveals much about the absolute uniqueness of God, but particularly about the saving relationship He has with His people: They are special to Him, and He is always faithful to them.

Third, the Lord is righteous. Daniel prayed, "O Lord, righteousness belongeth unto thee" (9:7), and then asked that the Lord would turn His anger away from His people "according to all thy righteousness" (9:16). He prayed this after admitting that the chastisement had come upon the people according to that same righteousness: "for the LORD our God is righteous in all his works which he doeth" (9:14). Righteousness refers essentially to God's conformity to His own infinite, eternal, and unchangeable perfections. Simply speaking, that God is righteous means He cannot be anything other than He is nor do anything other than He does. Whatever God does is right because God is God. God is incapable of doing anything except what is holy, just, good, and true.

Fourth, the Lord is merciful. This, too, is expressly stated in the prayer: "To the Lord our God belong mercies and forgivenesses" (9:9). Here the word "mercies" is different from the word translated "mercy" in verse four, which expresses God's covenant faithfulness. The word in verse nine refers to God's compassion and pity that moves Him to help those in desperate need. In this context, it refers specifically to His compassion that meets the need of the repentant sinner: He forgives. That the words "mercies" and "forgivenesses" occur in the plural indicates a Hebrew intensification of the concepts: There is abundant mercy and forgiveness with the Lord. Knowing this motivates prayer. The simple truth is that the more we know the Lord, the more we will pray. It is a sobering reality check to admit that the way we pray is always in proportion to our realization of how much we need and depend on the Lord. Prayerlessness invariably evidences self-dependence.

PRAYER INVOLVES CONFESSION

Daniel and the Psalmist shared the same conviction and confidence: "If I regard iniquity in my heart, the Lord will not hear me: But verily God hath heard me; he hath attended to the voice of my prayer" (Psalm 66:18-19). True confession leads to certain forgiveness (1 John 1:9) and the open door into God's presence. Confession of sins, itself an element of prayer, is prerequisite to God's hearing and answering prayer. Expressions of contrition, shame, confusion, admission of guilt, and confession of the corporate sins of the nation occur repeatedly throughout Daniel's prayer. Until a person abandons self-confidence and self-righteousness and recognizes his unworthiness, he will be not to prompted to appeal for God's help and mercy. Prayer always flows from the sense of need and relies on the certainty that God will hear the prayer of confession and the petitions that follow from a pure heart.

PRAYER INVOKES GREAT THINGS FROM GOD

Too often prayer tends to be vague, general, and timid. There is something oddly safe in that kind of praying, because faith is hardly threatened by timid prayers. So often we pray in such general terms that answers to the prayers are neither discernible nor deniable. "Be with the missionaries." That's safe. But the simple fact is that we have not because we ask not (James 4:2). The prayer of faith specifically asks from the Lord what needs to be asked. Daniel's prayer was to the point. Israel had justly suffered under divine displeasure because of sin (9:16). After confessing the sins, Daniel prayed that God would turn away His anger (9:16), show sympathy toward the nation's afflictions (9:18), and restore the blessing by causing His face to shine upon them (9:17). If the Lord did these things, Daniel could not doubt that He had heard and answered prayer. Asking the big things, however, does test the faith. The waiting time between the petition and answer creates a tension, but that tension should find relief in our resting on the promise that those who wait on the Lord will not be disappointed. The Lord said, "They shall not be ashamed that wait for me" (Isaiah 49:23). When we pray, we pray to a great God who is infinitely capable of doing great things. We might as well ask.

PRAYER APPEALS TO THE SUPREME MOTIVE

"Ye ask, and receive not, because ye ask amiss, that ye may consume it upon your lusts" (James 4:3). In praying, motive counts. Regardless of the specific petitions, Scriptural prayer always covets and promotes the glory of God. Daniel's prayer rejected any claim of personal merit as the basis for the granting of any petition (9:18); rather, Daniel prayed "for the Lord's sake" (9:17; see also v. 19) and "for thy great mercies" (9:18). God's honor was the preeminent objective; His great mercy, ultimately manifested in Christ, was the meritorious ground (see Isaiah 55:3 where Christ is designated as the "sure mercies of David"). That we pray in Jesus's name for Christ's sake ought not to be simply the jargon we use to Christianize prayer. It ought to be the sincere expression of a heart that will be happy with any way God answers prayer so long as He receives all the glory. God's glory as the supreme motive for prayer establishes the link between prayer and providence. Since the glory of God is the goal of providence, it is easy enough to see why God factors in the prayers of His people as a means of achieving that end.

THE MOVEMENT TO THE END

Gabriel, the messenger from the Lord and Daniel's interpreting angel, appeared to Daniel while he was praying and interrupted the prayer with God's gracious answer (9:20-23). Although Daniel lived many years before Paul expressed one of his inspired doxologies, I'm pretty sure that he concurred with the apostle's eloquent statement of praise: "Now unto him that is able to do exceeding abundantly above all that we ask or think...Unto him be glory in the church by Christ Jesus throughout all ages, world without end. Amen" (Ephesians 3: 20-21). Daniel prayed specifically for a restoration of Israel's position prior to the reversals of the exile years; God showed him that the end of the captivity was just another step in the progress of time leading to the certain coming of the long-promised Christ. The revelation of the "determined" Seventy Weeks (9:24) contributes irrefutable evidence supporting our thesis: God controls time.

I want to avoid all the speculation surrounding this vision and simply highlight the main points of the revelation. Three matters of interpretation regarding the weeks demand our attention: the symbolism of weeks, the arrangement of weeks, and the beginning and ending of the weeks.

THE SYMBOLISM

The first matter concerns the symbolism. Most scholars interpret the weeks to symbolize or represent weeks of years rather than weeks of days. Although ordinarily we would not refer to a week in terms of years, this construction is certainly feasible because the word translated "week" simply means a "unit of seven," most often a unit of seven days and hence a week. But these seventy weeks very probably signify seventy units of seven years each, for a total of 490 years.

THE ARRANGEMENT

The second matter pertains to the arrangement. The passage clearly divides the weeks into three segments: (1) one set of seven weeks, or 49 years; (2) one set of sixty-two weeks, or 434 years; and (3) one set of one week, or 7 years. Although the first seven weeks are isolated from the next sixty-two weeks, they seem to be consecutive, resulting in a total of 483 years for the first sixty-nine weeks. The last week (7 years) seems to be chronologically separated; certain events need to take place before it begins.

Recognizing this threefold arrangement is fairly easy; figuring out why the weeks are thus separated is perhaps not as simple. I think verse 25 explains why the first sixty-nine weeks are segmented. Although the arrival of Messiah the Prince is the ultimate focus, marking the end of the sixty-nine weeks, the text also issues the promise that the streets and walls of Jerusalem will be rebuilt. Remember that when Daniel received this vision, Jerusalem lay in ruins. Reversing those ruins was the particular topic of Daniel's prayer, and the text's isolation of the first seven weeks was a way to boldface God's specific answer to Daniel. It was part of God's promise for the city to be restored, and it eventually was. So two things were going to happen in the next 483 years: the city would be rebuilt and Messiah would come. Since the rebuilding of the city took place at the beginning of this period and the majority of waiting time for Messiah followed the restoration, the years were arranged to suggest that time disparity. At least, this is my guess as to why.

The last week is separated because the text is more concerned about what happens before the commencement of the last week than with how long it takes. Remember that prophetic texts quite commonly abandon sequential chronology in order to highlight epoch events. Verses 26 and 27 telescope the two key events that take place between the sixty-ninth and seventieth week: Messiah will die and the people of the prince will destroy Jerusalem. We detect no hint as to how much time lies between those two events. The seventieth week commences when that prince, the "Anti-Christ," enters into a covenant with the nation, ultimately leading to the infamous abomination of desolation.

Our concern at this point is not what the text says the Anti-Christ will do; we have already considered his opposition in the last chapter. Our concentration now is on what the text says Christ will do and has done. Daniel makes a direct statement about the vicarious sacrifice: "the Messiah (shall) be cut off, but not for himself" (9:26). Although being cut off obviously alludes to death, the expression "not for himself" has occasioned dispute. Some interpreters and versions suggest that when Messiah dies, He has nothing, an indication of His deep humility, extreme poverty, and even apparent failure. This interpretation has some warrant, but I prefer construing the statement to denote the atoning significance of that death: He died for our sins according to the Scripture. God's answer to Daniel was the gospel. It is regrettable that in interpreting the Seventy Weeks, people spend more time trying to figure out the identity of Anti-Christ than they do highlighting the person and work of Christ. Verse 24, which declares the sixfold purpose of the Seventy Weeks, reveals that it is all the work of Christ: finishing transgression, abolishing sin, atoning for iniquity, ushering in everlasting righteousness, validating and confirming every prophecy, and anointing the Most Holy.

THE TIMING

The third issue concerns the beginning and end of the weeks. Verse 25 marks the "going forth of the commandment to restore and to build Jerusalem" as the beginning of the 483-year period before the coming of Messiah. If we can figure out when that commandment was issued, we are in business. Four possibilities have presented themselves: (1) the initial decree of Cyrus in 538 B.C. (Ezra 1:1-4); (2) the renewal of Cyrus's decree by Darius in 520 B.C. (Ezra 6:6-12); (3) the decree of Artaxerxes concerning Ezra in 458 B.C. (Ezra 7:11-26); and (4) the decree of Artaxerxes to Nehemiah in 445 B.C. (Nehemiah 2:1-4).

Without going into all the arguments now, I'll state my preference for the fourth suggestion–the decree to Nehemiah–with its special focus on the streets and walls. Therefore, if we take into account some of the inherent difficulties with ancient calendar systems and that a prophetic year seemed to consist of only 360 days, the sixty-ninth week would have ended between A.D. 26 and 32. The prophetic precision is remarkable. Recall that the prophecy concerns Messiah's atoning death, not His birth. According to most chronologies, we would date the crucifixion of Christ at about A.D. 30, well within the prophetic projection. His birth would have been before the end of the sixty-nine weeks (4 B.C.), His death immediately after.

When the seventieth week will begin, only God knows. It is during that final week that the Anti-Christ mounts his opposition. It is at the end of that final week that the Anti-Christ is judged by the glorious return of the Lord Jesus. Just as certainly as that week will begin, it will end. Just as Daniel prayed in anticipation of Jeremiah's prophecy, Simeon and Anna might very well have been counting Daniel's seventy weeks as they waited for the consolation and redemption of Israel to come. It is impossible for us to count down to the commencement of Week Seventy, but we can be absolutely certain that it will begin according to the eternal schedule, and it will end on time. Our ignorance of the timing should not diminish our expectation of its execution or keep us from using the same means of grace that Daniel used as he anticipated the approaching of the fullness of time in which Christ would come. Our praying for Christ's return will not alter the divinely determined moment of that coming, but it should express our "can't wait until He comes" desire: "Even so, come, Lord Jesus" (Revelation 22:20). ⸙

CHAPTER EIGHT

UP CLOSE AND PERSONAL

"All things work together for good to them that love God, to them who are the called according to his purpose." Romans 8:28 is one of the easiest verses in the Bible to apply to someone else, yet, one of the most difficult to give credence to in moments of personal crisis. Memories of its truth flash like neon when we ponder God's past faithfulness, but the present too easily obscures its relevance, which in reality remains constant regardless of circumstance. What we believe to be true wrestles with what we think is happening, and the tension between faith and sight spoils our peace. Believing in the absolute sovereignty of God as fact does not always equate with resting in it as a joyous way of life. Why is it that unbelief always seems to hold hands with belief, tagging along at every step? There's an old hymn of John Newton that expresses this struggle and offers good counsel:

> *Begone, unbelief; my Savior is near,*
> *And for my relief will surely appear;*
> *By prayer let me wrestle, and He will perform;*
> *With Christ in the vessel, I smile at the storm.*

Though dark be my way, since He is my guide,

'Tis mine to obey, 'tis His to provide;

Though cisterns be broken, and creatures all fail,

The word He has spoken shall surely prevail.

His love in time past forbids me to think

He'll leave me at last in trouble to sink;

Each sweet Ebenezer I have in review

Confirms His good pleasure to help me quite through.

Why should I complain of want or distress,

Temptation or pain? He told me no less;

The heirs of salvation, I know from His Word,

Through much tribulation must follow their Lord.

Since all that I meet shall work for my good,

The bitter is sweet, the medicine, food;

Though painful at present, 'twill cease before long;

And then, O how pleasant the conqueror's song!

How a theology of time affects life is the real test–not of its truth, but of our faith. Our attention in Daniel so far has been on the big picture of God's sovereign operation in time. We have focused on the Lord's government and manipulation of time to accomplish His redemptive purpose in Jesus Christ. Human regimes come and go according to Heaven's disposition, all working in sequence and in behind-the-scenes harmony to achieve the consummate coming of the Kingdom of God. His kingdom always is and in its fullest sense is coming. Nothing has frustrated or can alter God's perfect will, and in fact everything–even the opposition–serves to bring it to manifest reality. However, it is one thing to see the big picture; it is another to realize that the big picture is composed of many little elements of which even we are part. The big picture requires that all the little parts fit together. Significantly, Daniel in his divinely inspired theology of time blends the macroscopic view of divine providence with microscopic applications of its operation. He brings the issues of providence up close and makes them personal.

Daniel's own life testifies to God's personal interest in and control of his affairs. From his captivity to his favor and position within the pagan courts, to his protection in the lion's den, Daniel was conscious of the Lord's hand upon him. Regardless of his circumstance, Daniel never seemed to worry. He provides a good example for us all. (I suppose that's to be expected since he is, after all, the principal character throughout the narrative.) However, in addition to the testimony of his own life, Daniel relates three accounts of individuals with whom God deals specifically and who react either properly or improperly to the Lord's control of their personal circumstances. I want to survey these three stories and draw out the appropriate lessons. We all should be able to confess with the Psalmist, "My times are in thy hand" (Psalm 31:15). That is the personal application of time theology.

A STORY OF COURAGE

Daniel 3 records the remarkable courage of Shadrach, Meshach, and Abed-nego. As minor characters, they appear only in the first three chapters of the narrative. In the first two chapters, they are companions but obviously followers of Daniel. Willing to suffer the consequences of their obedience to the Lord, they do the right things, but they take their cues from Daniel. In chapter three, however, they are alone, and without Daniel's example or prodding, they demonstrate their strong faith and personal commitment to the will of God.

This familiar Bible story of the fiery furnace, set in a world system that was both ignorant of and hostile to truth, teaches us that we must stand firm and faithful regardless of the external pressures to compromise. Shadrach, Meshach, and Abed-nego teach us that the courage and resolve to stand firm comes from faith in God and His Word. Knowing that whatever happened in time was God's will enabled them to face their situation with confidence. It is that kind of total dependence on God that empowers believers to stand on the promises. If these three companions teach us anything about the theology of time, it is this: There is more to life than time. Every proper application of time theology operates with a view to eternity; this temporal life is not all there is.

Although the particular trial of Shadrach, Meshach, and Abed-nego was unique to them, it nonetheless illustrates the kind of problem faced by every generation of saints and guides us to the solution. Their absolute commitment to the Lord enabled them to resist the world's pressure and to rest upon the Lord.

The World's Pressures

This world is no friend of grace; it never has been. Yet in this hostile world is where God has placed His people, and this world is where God's people must live to serve and glorify Him. The world's mission is at odds with God's. Whereas God's objective in grace is to mature His people into conformity to the image of Christ, the world's natural course moves in the opposite direction (Ephesians 2:2-3). This incident in the life of Shadrach, Meshach, and Abed-nego outlines the ageless tactics used by the world to seduce believers to worldliness and worldly thinking.

First, conformity to the world is made attractive. The issue confronting the expatriated Hebrews centered on the grand statue of gold that Nebuchadnezzar had erected in his own honor (3:1). Learning from Daniel's interpretation of the colossus dream that he was the head of gold went to his head! What better way to publicize his golden headship than to erect an enormous statue of himself! Resting on a nine-foot base and extending ninety feet into the air, this more than life-size image very likely only approximated how much larger than life Nebuchadnezzar saw himself.

The unveiling of the statue provided an occasion for celebration and a cause for great pomp. The crowd consisted of a "who's who" of Babylonian VIPs: Celebrities were invited (3:2), and they were to lead the masses gathered from every part of the empire (3:4). There was even a great orchestra to provide music for the official ceremony (3:5). This was a national happening; just being there was an honor. The only price was bowing to the image at the sound of the musical cue.

The entire scene shows how acceptance and just being a part of something can prove almost irresistibly attractive. Nobody wants to be left out.

Second, nonconformity is made dangerous. In addition to the statue, the crowd, and the orchestra, a furnace of burning fire situated for all to see (3:6) supplied a powerful motive to comply with the state's demand. The smoke and flames billowing from the furnace threatened everyone to listen carefully for the music that signaled the appropriate time to pay homage to the image. Given Babylon's penchant for what we might regard as cruel and inhumane punishments, being burned alive was no idle threat. The smoke was enough to force the crowd to bow down in unison.

Without doubt, many bowed down thoughtlessly just because everybody else was doing it. More than likely, some bowed with less than reverential thoughts toward Nebuchadnezzar. They bowed, but they didn't mean it. Whether thoughtlessly, hypocritically, or sincerely, it is always safe and easy to follow the crowd. The crowd can tolerate insincerity but not independence, particularly that which is motivated by religious conviction based on biblical truth. The world tends to be intolerant of any who defy society's norms and refuse to go along because of adherence to biblical principles. Today's consequence for nonconformity to the world may not be death in an oven, but separation from the world always entails serious repercussions. Sadly, it is usually something far less intimidating than a fiery death that seduces Christians to compromise their professed convictions.

Third, nonconformity is made conspicuous. When the note sounded, everything went according to plan: "All the people, the nations, and the languages, fell down and worshipped the golden image that Nebuchadnezzar the king had set up" (3:7). Everybody there bowed except Shadrach, Meshach, and Abed-nego (3:8, 12). Standing alone was probably the greatest pressure of all to bend over like everybody else; the smoke from the furnace had to be plainly visible with no heads in the way to obscure the view. But the text gives no hint that the three had even a moment's doubt about their decision to stand. I can't help wondering, however, how easy it would have been to rationalize in their conspicuous solitude and to convince themselves that they could bow down and still please God. "If we burn in the furnace, there will be no other witness left in Babylon. Where is Daniel, anyway?" "We probably should bow down. After all, God has ordained human government, and He expects us to obey those in authority over us." "People may mistake our conviction for arrogant defiance, and we would lose our testimonies." "If we bow down, we'll be where the people are, and we can talk to them about the Lord." "Nobody knows us here. What would it hurt?" I obviously have gone far beyond the Scripture and have committed the hermeneutical error of psychologizing (speculating about the motives and thoughts of the characters). The fact that I could generate these excuses so easily says more about me than about Shadrach, Meshach, and Abed-nego. The point is clear enough: it is hard to stand alone.

The Believer's Courageous Faith

Convinced of principles of truth and righteousness more important than life itself, Shadrach, Meshach, and Abed-nego took a courageous stand. Courage in and of itself is not a uniquely spiritual virtue, but when that courage flows from an unwavering conviction of the unchangeable truth of God's word and from a personal resolve to take God at His word, it becomes a virtue that is spiritual indeed. I suppose this kind of spiritual courage is nothing else than walking by faith. And every Christian is capable of it because faith's power comes from what is believed. Bear in mind that the value of faith is in its object, not in its exercise. All things are possible through faith because with God all things are possible. Faith, therefore, is not the psyching up of self with positive thoughts of "I can do it" or "I think I can," but the resting on God's faithfulness and might. This familiar story suggests some important lessons for every Christian concerning how to walk in time with courageous faith.

First, courageous faith is based on God's word. This principle is crucial if we are going to stand well in the times of crisis. The petty preferences and personal opinions that Christians are so often ready to fight over are ultimately without significance and will not in the end generate the kind of godly courage evidenced by the three Hebrews. Proud stubbornness can not be confused with spiritual conviction. Shadrach, Meshach, and Abed-nego were guided and ruled by God's word. They knew the Word well enough and had enough spiritual discernment to interpret the king's demand for what it really was. This ecumenical celebration was more than a political rally to salute the flag or to express their allegiance to Nebuchadnezzar. Their submission and loyalty to the state would not have been a contended issue; they rightly understood the command to bow down and worship the image to have religious overtones. Connecting it to Babylonian paganism, they interpreted the commanded gesture as idolatry (3:12). God's word forbade the worship of any other god (the First Commandment), and they could not nor would not pay homage to the statue regardless of the pressure placed on them. Obedience to God's word was not optional. Obedience is always the necessary corollary to faith.

Second, courageous faith operates regardless of the consequences. The response to their act of faith came immediately. The first response was the malicious anger expressed by the Chaldeans. Although the entire crowd was supposed to bow when the music sounded and only Shadrach, Meshach, and Abed-nego remained standing, somebody in the crowd must have been peeking, because some of the Chaldeans knew what had happened. When they found out, they "accused the Jews" (3:8) and tattled to the king (3:9). A more literal translation of the Aramaic of verse 8 expresses something of the spiteful vehemence of the Chaldeans: "they ate the pieces of the Jews." This idiom parallels ours of chewing somebody out or up one side and down the other. The ungodly tend to hate what they do not understand. Since the refusal to bow was a spiritual issue, the Babylonians could not comprehend why the Jews stood defiantly against the crowd. All they could do was interpret the behavior as strange, anti-social, and unBabylonian. Nobody enjoys being chewed out, misunderstood, ridiculed, or hated. But the three Hebrews knew that God's cause was more important than personal feelings.

The second response involved the opportunity for a second chance (3:13-18). Nebuchadnezzar, notwithstanding his self-absorption, was merciful enough to give the Jews the benefit of the doubt. He assumed that their behavior was due to their misunderstanding, so he explained the whole procedure again. What appeared to be the king's patience was just another avenue of testing. It is a common ploy of Satan to bring into question the results of faithful obedience. So far the only thing achieved by their stand was to incite the anger of everybody who knew about their stand: upon re-evaluation, maybe defying the command was not the best course of behavior. But that option never crossed their minds. The visible results of trusting and obeying God must not be factors in motivating those who are committed to the Lord. We are to trust and obey for the sake of trusting and obeying; there is no other way.

Third, courageous faith is neither obnoxious nor presumptuous. The three faced the consequences of their decision without arrogance toward the king and without presumption before the Lord. When confronted by Nebuchadnezzar, they simply and respectfully acknowledged that the indictment against them was accurate and that there was no need to offer any defense (3:16). They were firm but not defiant, following, before the fact, the example of Christ, "who before Pontius Pilate witnessed a good confession" (1 Timothy 6:13). Too often, some Christians, while taking the right stand on issues, do so in such a self-righteous and arrogant manner that even other Christians who agree with them want to disassociate themselves. Being cantankerous only harms the cause.

Even more outstanding to me than their humility before Nebuchadnezzar was their sure confidence in God's will, even though they did not know how the plan of the divine will would come together for them. They just knew it had to be good and right. God's ability to deliver them from the king's furnace was not in doubt. They knew He could; but they did not know if He would (3:17-18). They were willing to risk their lives, certain that whatever happened would be the good and perfect will of God. That kind of commitment is not natural; it is the operation of faith.

I emphasize that their willingness to see God's will accomplished regardless of what happened to them personally makes this narrative a first-rate example of the application of time theology. Faith in the good providence of God invariably strengthens the performance of obedient duty. They had the assurance that their times were in the hand of God and He would use them well to glorify Himself. That is true for us all. What could be better than that?

GOD'S UNFAILING PURPOSE

One way or another, God achieves His glory and His people's good, but He doesn't always do it the way we might expect. The accomplishing of that purpose for Shadrach, Meshach, and Abed-nego did not mean preventing adversity: they were thrown alive into the fire (3:19-23). Nebuchadnezzar had become so enraged against the three that he gave orders to stoke the flames, intensifying the heat as much as possible. So hot was the furnace that the heat fatally scorched the would-be executioners, and I'm fairly certain that as the three were being cast into the fire, they thought that their time was up and that they would soon be in the presence of their Lord. This bit of irony highlights the amazing nature of the rest of the story.

Although it was the will of God to place His servants in the furnace, it was not His will to leave them alone. Regardless of how horrific the circumstances, God has promised His presence to be the constant company of His people. Shadrach, Meshach, and Abed-nego were wrong about their time being up, but they were right about their being soon in the presence of their Lord. What Isaiah prophesied figuratively, the three Hebrews experienced most literally: "When thou passest through the waters, I will be with thee; and through the rivers, they shall not overflow thee; when thou walkest through the fire thou shalt not be burned; neither shall the flame kindle upon thee" (43:2). They were not burned, and the Lord was genuinely with them.

When Nebuchadnezzar looked into the furnace, he witnessed Isaiah 43:2 in operation. Although the now dead executioners had tossed three bound men into the flames, the astonished king saw four men walking around as though they were strolling in a park, giving no sign of fear or pain. The fourth man really caught the king's attention, and he exclaimed, "The form of the fourth is like the Son of God" (3:25). This statement raises two questions: (1) Whom did Nebuchadnezzar see? (2) Whom did Nebuchadnezzar think he saw?

Let me answer the second question first. The Aramaic expression translates literally "a son of gods." Semitic language often uses the word "son" to designate members of a class. This would mean that Nebuchadnezzar recognized the fourth individual as belonging to the class of supernatural beings, a designation that fits with his referring to the individual as an "angel" in verse 28. As a pagan, Nebuchadnezzar would not have had a clue about the Second Person of the Trinity, but the sight was so glorious that even a pagan could recognize that this was someone supernatural.

Now to the first question. I believe that Nebuchadnezzar saw the Second Person of the Trinity in Christophany, a pre-incarnate appearance of the Lord Jesus Christ. Although Nebuchadnezzar saw Him, the Lord did not appear primarily for his benefit; He was there for the comfort and encouragement of the three who had been faithful to Him unto what they perceived to be their death. The Lord's presence may not always be—and usually is not—evident to the natural sight, but it is always the reality of faith.

Whereas the Lord's presence with His people is a guaranteed promise, physical deliverance from danger is not (see Hebrews 11: 36-38). In this incident, however, it was the Lord's will to deliver. Although not naming Shadrach, Meshach, and Abed-nego specifically, Hebrews 11:34 mentions those who by faith "quenched the violence of fire." The Lord's deliverance was remarkable and complete. When all was done, those rescued from the fire did not even smell of smoke (3:27). God loosed them from their bonds (3:25), comforted them in their trial (3:24, 25, 28), protected them from harm (3:27), and honored them before their previous accusers, causing them to prosper (3:30). In this instance, spectacular deliverance was the best way for God to receive glory. Proud Nebuchadnezzar was forced to admit concerning the God of Shadrach, Meshach, and Abed-nego that "there is no other God that can deliver after this sort," and he made it a crime throughout his kingdom to blaspheme this God (3:29). What started as a solitary witness to the one true and living God by three seemingly insignificant young men in the plain of Dura spread by the decree of a pagan king to the whole realm. This is an undisputed example of God's using the wrath of man to get praise for Himself (Psalm 76:10).

I suppose many of us have flannelgraph figures of the fiery furnace etched in our memories from our days in Sunday school when we learned about the importance of resisting peer pressure. That is an important lesson for Christians of any age. But the lessons from this long familiar story are not limited to childhood and are most relevant to our principal theme. A biblical view of time means that we willingly submit our personal times to the hand of God, trusting that whatever He chooses to do with our times is right and good for us.

A STORY OF CONVERSION

Daniel 4 records a striking transformation in the personal life of Nebuchadnezzar. Nebuchadnezzar was a head of state and therefore a public man. But even public figures are private souls who are individually accountable before God. My opinion is that Nebuchadnezzar's transformation was more than a mere behavioral reformation or attitude adjustment; it was, rather, a spiritual conversion of his soul. The conversion of sinners in time is always up close and personal; God saves sinners individually, not corporately. Even though every conversion is unique, nonetheless a common pattern does operate. A story of conversion integrally relates to a theology of time because very simply, if sinners are to be saved, they must be saved in time. Of all that takes place in life's time between birth and death, nothing is of more eternal consequence than personal conversion. Nebuchadnezzar's unique testimony suggests three things common to every genuine conversion: need, divine intervention, and profession.

Before highlighting some of the truths from this story, I need to offer a little explanation about the order of events in chapter 4. The sequence is potentially confusing unless we recognize that almost the whole chapter is Nebuchadnezzar's own testimony after his conversion. The chapter begins with a doxology in retrospect of what God has done (4: 1-3). This is followed by a detailed account of the dream and Daniel's interpretation and warning to the king (4:4-27) which preceded his conversion. The inspired narrator (Daniel) then interrupts to record the actualization of what was dreamed (4:28-33), and the chapter ends with Nebuchadnezzar's first-person profession of faith (4:34-37). With this in mind, we can discover the key lessons about conversion.

PRE-CONVERSION PRIDE

"Is not this great Babylon, that I have built for the house of the kingdom by the might of my power, and for the honour of my majesty?" (4:30). The greatness of Babylon was undeniable. Modern archaeologists still marvel over the architectural genius and magnificence of the Babylon that Nebuchadnezzar had built. How much more its ancient residents and visitors would have been impressed with this queen of all cities. With its seemingly impregnable walls, the imposing Ishtar Gate, the grand temples, the lavish palace, and the wonder of the hanging gardens, Babylon's splendor was unrivalled. From the perspective of natural sight, Nebuchadnezzar had every reason to be proud of his accomplishments.

Nothing, however, can be concluded from natural sight alone. Daniel had made it explicitly clear to Nebuchadnezzar at the beginning of his reign that "the God of heaven hath given thee a kingdom, power, and strength, and glory" (2:37). In his conceit, Nebuchadnezzar took credit for it all. At this point, he had none of Solomon's spiritual insight. Solomon, whose glory and building projects exceeded even Nebuchadnezzar's, confessed after examining all that he had accomplished, "Behold, all was vanity and vexation of spirit, and there was no profit under the sun" (Ecclesiastes 2:11). His achievements were nothing apart from the Lord, who gave him the necessary gifts to do what he did. Nebuchadnezzar, on the other hand, resting and flourishing in his palace (4:4), was the image of Jeremiah's cursed man "that trusteth in man, and maketh flesh his arm, and whose heart departeth from the Lord" (Jeremiah 17:5).

Although Nebuchadnezzar's manifestation of pride was unique, his self-absorbing pride is the common and fatal malady of all sinners, whether prosperous or poor, achievers or nonachievers. The unchanging spiritual law is that God "resisteth the proud, and giveth grace to the humble" (1 Peter 5:5). Nebuchadnezzar stood in need of grace. Unless the Lord intervened and changed his heart, Nebuchadnezzar's prosperous time would surely lead to a tragic eternity. So it is for every sinner: Divine intervention is necessary to change time's destination.

DIVINE INTERVENTION

Conversion is marked by faith toward God and repentance from sin: It is the first conscious response to the grace of God that irresistibly invades the heart, implanting spiritual life and enabling spiritual perception. The story of Nebuchadnezzar's conversion puts a face on Paul's theological propositions that "faith cometh by hearing, and hearing by the word of God" (Romans 10:17) and that "there is no difference between the Jew and the Greek: for the same Lord over all is rich unto all that call upon him" (Romans 10:12). The Lord graciously gave the word and governed the circumstances that led the pagan king to salvation.

First, the Lord gave the word through a dream, a common means of God's communication to sinners in that dispensation. Without spiritual life or perception, however, Nebuchadnezzar had no idea what the dream meant, only that it was troubling (4:5). God intended grace for Nebuchadnezzar, and He insured that everything would be in place for the temporal execution of that grace. Among the reasons God had sovereignly brought Daniel to Babylon was to position the necessary preacher for the conversion of the proud king. Again Paul's inspired theology explains the means God uses to save sinners: "How then shall they call on him in whom they have not believed? and how shall they believe in him of whom they have not heard? and how shall they hear without a preacher? And how shall they preach, except they be sent?" (Romans 10:14-15a). Since God is both the Author and the Finisher of faith (Hebrews 12:2), there is never any chance that some essential component of the means of grace will fail to achieve the end or purpose of grace. God controls and governs time with a view to His eternal purpose, including His purpose to save individuals, whose salvation is always to praise of the glory of His grace (see Ephesians 1:4-12).

Since God resists the proud and gives grace to the humble, He had to humble proud Nebuchadnezzar to awaken within him his need for grace. Only as sinners are brought to the end of themselves are they moved to recognize the Lord. In the dream, the Lord revealed to the king the path of humiliation, and Daniel interpreted and applied the word. Here are the salient points of the dream and their relevance. He saw a flourishing tree large and fruitful enough to provide sustenance for all the creatures of earth (4:10). But then the tree was chopped down to a stump (4:14-15). Strangely, the stump was fettered and abandoned to the elements of nature (4:15). And even more strangely, the stump was changed into a beast, destined to live off the grass of the field for a period of seven times (4:15-16). When Daniel learned the details of the dream, he knew it was going to be a hard message to deliver, but he faithfully delivered it in spite of its foreboding message. He told Nebuchadnezzar that the tree represented the rise of his empire and his personal majesty (4:22). The chopping down of the tree and the remaining of a stump represented God's intent to remove the exercise of sovereignty from Nebuchadnezzar personally, forcing him to live like an ox for a period of seven times, most likely seven years (4:23-25). Daniel made it clear that God was lowering him in order to bring him to his spiritual senses (4:24-26). Like any good preacher, Daniel gave the word and pressed his one-man congregation to repent while there was time: "Wherefore, O king, let my counsel be acceptable unto thee, and break off thy sins by righteousness, and thine iniquities by shewing mercy to the poor; if it may be a lengthening of thy tranquillity" (4:27).

Second, God governed the circumstances to achieve His purpose. A year passed after the dream with no evidence of repentance. But in His own time, the Lord in mercy intervened, and Daniel 4:28 effectively sums it up: "All this came upon the king Nebuchadnezzar." At the very moment the king was bragging, a voice from heaven interrupted, and the humiliation process began. To put it simply, Nebuchadnezzar lost his mind. God drove him crazy. It seems as though the once glorious monarch thought he was a cow, and all that his royal herdsmen could do was to tie him up in the backyard of the palace and let him do what cows do. We can only wonder how the court's "spin doctors" handled this situation for seven years. While the administration undoubtedly kept this a secret from the public, God secured the kingdom for the insane king (4:26), but more significantly He was having his way in Nebuchadnezzar's heart. At the appropriate moment, the king lifted his "cow" eyes to heaven and realized what he never had before in his previously rational state: God rules (4:34). The only feasible explanation for this transition from irrationality to spiritually rational understanding is the gracious intervention of God. Without such divine interference every sinner is doomed; with it sinners are wondrously converted.

Remember Daniel's representation of Nebuchadnezzar and his kingdom as a winged lion whose wings were plucked and who received the heart of a man (7:4). I think what Daniel visualized occurred in time in the event described in chapter 4. The irony is noteworthy. In vision, Daniel saw the beast humanized. In fact, the humanizing of the beast was accomplished by the bestializing of the human. The point to learn is this: When God has purposed to save a sinner, He does all that is necessary to save that sinner. In one way or another He always works through conviction and circumstance to bring the sinner to his sense of spiritual need. His purpose never fails; God's plans always come together.

POST-CONVERSION PROFESSION

Daniel 4 is the last record we have of Nebuchadnezzar. Exactly when his conversion occurred is impossible to date, but very probably it was toward the end of his career. The Scripture does not preserve for us the details of how his life changed. It does, however, record for us his profession of faith. One of the evidences of saving grace is the ability to comprehend spiritual truth (1 Corinthians 2:10-14). Again according to Paul in Romans 10, one of the conditions of salvation is confessing with the mouth that Jesus is Lord (verse 9). After his humiliation and spiritual awakening, Nebuchadnezzar uttered a mouth confession of unquestionable orthodoxy concerning the absolute Lordship of the God of heaven (4:34-35, 37). Daniel had expressed this truth to Nebuchadnezzar at the beginning (chapter 2), but the truth was without effect in an unresponsive heart. As a pagan and polytheist, Nebuchadnezzar was at times willing to salute Daniel's God for revealing secrets (2:47) or the God of Shadrach, Meshach, and Abed-nego for rescuing from fire (3:29). Polytheists were quite happy to say "uncle" when somebody else's god showed some superiority. But the confession in chapter 4 goes beyond saying "uncle." When God changed the heart, the truth took hold, and the mouth opened in humble praise and willing submission. Nebuchadnezzar acknowledged the Most High God as the one true and living God whose sovereign authority both in heaven and on earth was eternal, incontestable and irresistible and whose works were always right and just. That is quite a creed. It is a creed, by the way, that not only gives evidence of a regenerated heart, but also highlights the elements of truth essential for defining a theology of time.

Nebuchadnezzar's conversion illustrates another dimension of God's sovereign control over men, their circumstances, and their times. On one level, God used Nebuchadnezzar and his empire as an instrument in His own hand to accomplish His own purpose. Nebuchadnezzar was a key player in the big picture. On another level, God dealt with Nebuchadnezzar as an ordinary sinner in need of saving grace. God took one who was His servant in time and made him His child for eternity.

A STORY OF CONDEMNATION

Daniel 5 chronicles the last few hours of the time allotted to Belshazzar. Its instruction regarding sin and its consequences illustrates the folly of not learning the lessons taught by time in time. Although designated "the king of the Chaldeans" (5:30), Belshazzar was not a particularly significant figure from either the secular or the sacred perspective. For hundreds of centuries after his death, Daniel's was the only known record that he even existed. Archaeology has unearthed a few references that explain his co-regency with Nabonidus, but even the secular records make plain his minor political status as a secondary figure who administered the affairs of the city during the frequent absences of Nabonidus. He had position without ultimate power. Living in luxury, he probably had more time on his hands than he knew what to do with. Daniel 5, however, makes it gravely clear that he didn't have as much time as he thought. But then, nobody does.

The transition from the Babylonian kingdom to the Medo-Persian kingdom was an integral component in the big picture of God's plan, revealing His kingdom and leading to His Christ. This up close and personal glimpse of the last moments of Belshazzar's life reveals how minutely and complexly God has orchestrated the affairs of time to accomplish all of His purposes. If I can use a familiar adage, God is well able "to kill two birds with one stone." His execution of the big plan included the execution of Belshazzar. Just as God's distribution of saving grace is always individually personal, so is the dispersing of His justice. If Nebuchadnezzar's personal story gives hope to sinners, Belshazzar's issues a warning. Belshazzar's is a story of condemnation.

A MOMENTARY PLEASURE

Belshazzar's legacy is tragic. Although Daniel uses him on two occasions simply as a calendar to date visions (7:1 and 8:1), the only information giving any insight into his character or contributions concerns a drunken celebration that ends in death. He planned a banquet and invited a thousand state officials along with his wives and concubines (5:1-4). Since official state affairs did not normally include women on the invitation list, their presence indicates that this was not a time for business; it was, rather, party time. It wasn't long before the wine started flowing freely, and one thing began to lead to another. Soon the crowd was drunk, and we can only imagine the sensuous abandonment that occurred. From a worldly assessment, they were really having fun.

As so often occurs in sinful abandonment, the sins of the flesh express themselves in sacrilege against God. In his stupor, Belshazzar ordered his servants to bring in the holy vessels from the Temple in Jerusalem to be used as goblets for the continued profligacy of his drunken guests. Years earlier Nebuchadnezzar had transported these golden and silver vessels from Jerusalem to Babylon as part of his spoil of victory. Archiving these religious artifacts and displaying them as the evidence of Marduk's superiority over the gods of conquered peoples were normal procedure. But profaning them was not the norm. And particularly, the profaning of those items that had been consecrated to the one true and living God was a blasphemous and serious mistake. Belshazzar was so taken up by the thrill of the moment that he gave no thought to the eternal consequences of his temporal transgression. That is invariably one of the real dangers of sin. Sin serves the moment, but its pleasures are "only for a season" (Hebrews 11:25). Belshazzar was having the time of his life.

A MONUMENTAL PRONOUNCEMENT

Unexpectedly, the God whom Belshazzar mocked contributed to the celebration. Out of nowhere, fingers appeared writing a cryptic message on the wall (5:5). Although he was drunk, and drunken people sometimes see things that aren't really there, Belshazzar knew all too certainly that what he saw was real. He sobered up quickly (5: 6) and brought in his advisors to decipher the handwriting on the wall (5:7). For whatever reason, none of the wise men were able to read the message, let alone tell what it meant (5:8). When the queen heard about the quandary, she told Belshazzar about Daniel and recounted his extraordinary display of wisdom back in the days of Nebuchadnezzar (5:10-12). So Belshazzar sent for Daniel and offered him a significant reward for reading and interpreting the message, including promotion to the third rank in the kingdom (5:16). That would place Daniel right after Belshazzar, who was second after Nabonidus. My guess is that Daniel had already read the message to himself and was, therefore, quick to turn down the offer (5:17). Being third in line that night was not a particularly attractive place to be.

He did agree, however, to read and interpret the message to the distraught king, but not before preaching a little sermon. Daniel always insisted that the Lord's word be accompanied by application. He took as "the text" for this sermon God's sovereign and gracious dealings with Nebuchadnezzar (5:18-21). He recounted how God at first had given the kingdom and glory to Nebuchadnezzar and how He at last humiliated the king in order to bring him to the personal knowledge of truth. Nebuchadnezzar had gotten the point, but Belshazzar did not, even though he knew the story: "And thou his son, O Belshazzar, hast not humbled thine heart, though thou knewest all this" (5:22). In fact, in spite of what he knew, he lifted himself up against the Lord, refusing to glorify "the God in whose hand" his breath was (5:23). Belshazzar failed to learn this vital lesson from history: His times were in God's hand. That is a sobering thought in light of the theme we have been developing throughout this study: Our times are in His hands as well. So may God help us to learn the lessons from "His story."

Having directed Belshazzar's attention to the absolute sovereignty of God, Daniel turned to the handwriting on the wall. Ironically, even the location of the writing may have served to boldface the message itself. We know from excavations of various ancient palaces that the walls were often decorated with reliefs depicting the exploits and conquests of the regime. That the Lord wrote the message of doom over the record of triumph signed that those temporal achievements were nothing in comparison to the more weighty issues of eternity. God's works always override man's.

The word of condemnation was brief but powerful: "MENE, MENE, TEKEL, UPHARSIN" (5:25). I've often wondered why the wise men of Babylon could not read this when even my beginning Aramaic students have little trouble parsing and crudely translating the text: "Having been counted, having been counted, having been weighed, and having been divided." That's crude, but that's essentially what it says. After he read it, Daniel did not translate it, but he did give the grim interpretation (5:26-28). He interpreted the "MENE" to mean that God had numbered the days of Belshazzar's reign, and the number was up. "TEKEL" meant that God had weighed the king, and he failed to balance the scales. "PERES" (the singular form of UPHARSIN) meant that the Medes and Persians would take the kingdom. It is interesting that "MENE" and "TEKEL" are both singular forms, whereas "UPHARSIN" is plural. I think the significance of this is that the first two are directed to Belshazzar personally, whereas the last refers to the empire corporately. Of course, once the personal words were fulfilled, what happened to the kingdom would be of no consequence to the king, but the phrasing emphasizes again how all at once God addressed both the big and the little pictures of His purpose. The big picture would continue according to plan; there was still time to come. But unhappily in regard to Belshazzar's little place in the picture, time was about to end.

AN IMMEDIATE PUNISHMENT

No time was wasted in fulfilling the wall's portent. Daniel 5:30 ominously says it all: "In that night was Belshazzar the king of the Chaldeans slain." There is not a word here that is difficult to understand, and I can add nothing to it.

A night that started with a king's party ended with the king's departure from this life. I don't know how old Belshazzar was when he was slain, but I'm almost certain that when that night began, he had no idea it would be his last. He no doubt thought he had plenty of time left, if he thought about it at all. I'm fairly sure about this because that's the way natural men tend to think. The Psalmist described the thinking of the wicked like this: "Their inward thought is, that their houses shall continue for ever, and their dwelling places to all generations" (49: 11). Death is always something that happens to others, and somehow people can easily convince themselves that they will be the grand exception to what they see happening to others. But the Bible is explicit that it is a human thing to die (Hebrews 9:27). Only God knows the date, time, and place of that appointment, but notwithstanding our ignorance of those details, it will be an appointment that we will not miss.

If Belshazzar's last night on earth teaches us anything relevant to our theology of time, it is that we must take advantage of the time we have to make sure that we are right with God. Since we do not know the eternally scheduled time of our deaths, it is imperative that we be ready for it whenever it comes. What we do in time regarding our relationship with God fixes our place in eternity. I can't help thinking of the words to a hymn whose author is now anonymous, but whose message is most pointed.

> *Life at best is very brief,*
> *Like the falling of a leaf,*
> *Like the binding of a sheaf:*
> *Be in time.*
> *Fleeting days are telling fast*
> *That the die will soon be cast,*
> *And the fatal line be passed:*
> *Be in time.*

I suppose of all that we have considered about the unfailing purpose of God, what we have taken into account in this chapter is in many ways the most important. Until the truth of the providence of

God becomes personal, it remains nothing more than doctrinal theory. Divine providence is not to be debated; it is to be enjoyed. Too often we are content to examine truth without appropriating it to ourselves by faith. Ecclesiastes 9:1 declares "that the righteous, and the wise, and their works, are in the hand of God." That ought to be a truth of comfort and consolation to every believer: No believer is excluded. The kind of direct, divine superintendence evidenced in the stories of Shadrach, Meshach, Abed-nego, and Nebuchadnezzar remains true for us. They are just examples of God's up close and personal interest and control, given to us as illustration of the Lord's norm and to set a pattern for how we should react to God's acts in our behalf.

But no unbeliever is excluded, either. So the kind of direct, divine superintendence evidenced in the story of Belshazzar also remains true for the lost. His story stands as sobering warning of the Lord's norm in dealing with sinners who live oblivious to His control. What is a source of comfort to saints should be a source of concern for sinners. But so long as there is time, there is hope even for sinners: "For to him that is joined to all the living there is hope" (Ecclesiastes 9:4). ⊰⊱

CONCLUSION

I began by asking two questions: How goes the world? How goes life? In the several months that have passed since I wrote the introduction to this book, much has happened both in the world and in my life. The world has been in and out of war and has been threatened by the outbreak of a mysterious disease. Together, that war and that disease have claimed the lives of thousands, all of whom were alive with some sense of future when I asked the questions the first time. My own life as it touches family, friends, health, and work has experienced changes that I could not have anticipated when I started this project–some pleasant and some not. During these several months, life has progressed as it always has, from crisis to crisis. Things have changed, but nothing is different. Who is in control? Is anyone?

My objective in this little book has been to answer those questions, and the answer is really quite simple. The God of heaven controls everything, and everything in the world generally and in life specifically goes according to His eternal will and His temporal operation. As simple and as biblical as this answer is, the answer itself often raises further questions and causes conflicts in our heads, if not our hearts. Too often what we don't know whittles away at what we do. Ignorance about the "why's" of life or the "what's" of the future can easily produce anxiety, feelings of uncertainty, and questions about the ultimate realities and meaning of life. Sooner or later something inevitably happens that seemingly does not match our knowledge of God's goodness and justice, and we face the dilemma of doctrine's conflict with experience. When experience grapples with doctrine, two alternatives arise: (1) interpreting experience in the light of doctrine, or (2) changing doctrine to conform to experience. The first is the operation of reasonable faith; the second is the operation of faithless reason. Faith is never unreasonable, but it often rests in that which is beyond reason, that is, beyond our individual capacities to explain. The most reasonable thing we can do is to trust God even–and perhaps I should say especially–about the issues of time and life that we do not understand.

In many ways, I am the most unqualified person I know of to write on the subject of living by faith in the absolute sovereignty of God and the unfailing execution of His purposes. Those who know me well may think it somewhat hypocritical for me to address this topic and to admonish others to walk by faith. Worry never seems far away from me. Sometimes when I'm not worrying, I catch myself and wonder what it is I've forgotten. My wife, who seems never to worry, has often said that I'm not happy unless I'm worrying about something. Perhaps she's right. My concerns are always unfounded. I do not entertain any doubt concerning the facts of the matter. The Lord has given me a greater measure of knowledge than faith. I know without doubt that God has decreed the end from the beginning and that He uses all that He has set in place in time to accomplish His good and perfect will. I know that there is nothing better for me than God's good and perfect will. I know, therefore, that there is no legitimate reason to worry about anything. But what I know and what I do with what I know are not always the same. In retrospect, I cannot see one instance in my life that has made me wonder whether God worked things together for good. My mental diary is full of entries that now make sense and bear witness to the Lord's faithfulness. Here's my problem. Although I believe unequivocally that God will ultimately accomplish the good He has promised, sometimes I think too much about all the means that God may use to accomplish His "up close and personal" end for me. I tend to worry about all the "what ifs" of the immediate future. These "what ifs" too easily distract me from reasonable faith and pilfer the peace of mind that is supposed to surpass understanding. So I am not writing as a hypocrite, for I make no false claims. I am not a bystander to the problem; I write as one who knows firsthand the tension of faith and who needs to live in the reality of truth. It is my confession that I believe. It is my prayer that the Lord will help my unbelief.

I have addressed this constant issue of life in terms of a theology of time. Time is where we live; what happens in time is all that experientially we know. If anything is true about a personal, vital, and saving relationship with God in Christ, it is that that relationship defines every sphere of life. There is no part of life that can be divorced from theology—what we know of God. A theology of time, therefore, simply integrates our knowledge of God into life. We must interpret all of time, including our own, in the light of God. Time changes, but God does not. He is the one constant in all the vicissitudes of life.

The Book of Daniel has been our casebook for study. Daniel is our guide to understanding time. Although the doctrine of God's sovereign rule of time, circumstance, and individual lives pervades all of Scripture, it is the principal theme of Daniel. Daniel is a book of history, surveying time from Daniel's own moment to the consummation of time. In a most remarkable and obvious way, Daniel outlines history as "His story." As Daniel tells "His story," he provides us an inspired philosophy of history, a godly worldview, and in other words, a theology of time. He does not record everything that is going to happen everywhere at every point of time, but he details enough to justify the conclusion that everything that does happen must be understood as an integral part of the progress of "His story." To study Daniel's message is to follow this prophet to an understanding of time.

Unfortunately, and far too frequently, the book suffers from the sensationalism of those who isolate the final installments of Daniel's timeline without consideration of the whole course. They reduce the book to a crystal ball unveiling the end of the world in terms of strange symbols that come to light again and again in whatever may be the focus of current events. Such sensationalism misses the point of prophecy generally and of Daniel specifically. This is one reason there are no pictures of monsters on the cover of my book–the usual way of advertising Daniel. Undeniably, Daniel predicts the end times in certain terms, and all of us naturally entertain some interest in the last days. But Daniel's purpose in his detailed eschatology was not to satisfy curiosity about the future but to engender peace of mind for the present. Knowing that God controls the future irrefutably proves that God controls the present. It was proof for those living in Daniel's day as well as for all those who would live from Daniel's day until the future itself becomes present. It functions, therefore, as proof for us who live in one of the "in-between" periods on Daniel's chart of history. God expects us to think and to make the necessary deductions from His word. Since God has controlled the past and determines the future, He manages all the in-betweens as well.

Daniel views time as the arena of God's providence wherein God governs everyone and everything according to His wisdom and good pleasure. What happens in time, whether past, present, or future, is the operation of God's unfailing plan. In "His story" according to Daniel, absolutely nothing is capable of frustrating or altering God's plan, and even the opposition that tries is part of the means God uses to achieve His objective. Daniel was neither a theological theorist nor a hypocrite. He preached what he practiced and practiced what he preached. His take on time would be foolishly idealistic were it not for the fact that Daniel himself lived in troubling times when it seemed that God had lost either control or interest in what was happening. In Daniel's time ungodly regimes ruled the world, and the remnant of God's people was a persecuted minority. And just to keep things in perspective, Daniel predicted that "there shall be a time of trouble, such as never was" (12: 1). Although time would progress from bad to worse and from crisis to crisis, it would progress according to God's plan and therefore on schedule and on course. By prophecy and by history, Daniel made it clear that everything was okay; there was no cause to worry.

What Daniel taught through his inspired history, Solomon taught through his divinely inspired worldview or philosophy of life. In fact, I referred to Solomon's masterful explanation of time in the Introduction, and I'm including in the appendices an article that I wrote some time ago that develops those ideas more thoroughly. What Daniel taught historically and what Solomon taught philosophically, Paul applies directly with apostolic authority. Listen to these convicting commands.

> Rejoice in the Lord alway: and again I say, Rejoice. Let your moderation be known unto all men. The Lord is at hand. Be careful for nothing; but in every thing by prayer and supplication with thanksgiving let your requests be made known unto God. And the

peace of God, which passeth all understanding, shall keep your hearts and minds through Christ Jesus. Finally, brethren, whatsoever things are true, whatsoever things are honest, whatsoever things are just, whatsoever things are pure, whatsoever things are lovely, whatsoever things are of good report; if there be any virtue, and if there be any praise, think on these things. Those things, which ye have both learned, and received, and heard, and seen in me, do: and the God of peace shall be with you. (Philippians 4:4-9)

Paul's admonishment to constant joy and peace is the outworking of a practical theology of time. That Paul issued these imperatives from prison reminds us that this happy contentment with life exists quite independent of life's circumstances. Paul knew that nothing in life could separate him from the love and presence of Christ (see Romans 8:35-39) and that nothing, therefore, could rob him of the contentment possible when faith overrides sight.

I want to conclude this whole study of time with a synopsis of Paul's formula for living peacefully in time with the God of peace. This text from Philippians 4 outlines four steps to being satisfied with whatever God brings into our times. Paul, like Daniel, becomes our guide because he says to do what he has taught not just by precept but also by personal example (4:9).

First, rejoice in the Lord (4:4). The word "rejoice" involves contentment and satisfaction. It is more of an attitude of heart and frame of mind than a facial expression. Its secret is found in its locus: the Lord. Circumstances change; prosperity and adversity travel the same street. But the Lord is changeless, and our relationship with God in Christ is unalterable. We can lose the stuff of life that may from time to time put a smile on the face, but we can never lose

Christ, the Source and Reason of true joy (see Habakkuk 3:17-18 for a similar thought). If we are not content with Christ, we will have no defense against the depression or fear caused by the norms of life. But if our delight is truly in the Lord, it is absolutely impossible to be disappointed, because He will always give us the desires of our heart. He will give us Himself (Psalm 37:4).

Second, reveal selflessness to others (4:5). The Authorized Version translates, "let your moderation be known unto all men." At first glance this injunction seems irrelevant to our theme of time, but in reality it is very much to the point. The sense of the word "moderation" includes the notions of forbearance, patience, gentleness, or good will; it expresses the idea of selflessness. Discontentment generally flows from self-absorption. When the issues of time, circumstance, and interpersonal relationships are measured against the standard of self, only what appears to benefit self gratifies. Selfishness is natural, so the Christian virtue of unselfishness is a mark of grace. We must not interpret time just from the narrow perspective of where we stand in it or of what is happening to us at any given moment. It is sobering to have to admit that "it's not all about us." But we are important parts of God's master plan. God has placed us where we are for His good purpose and for our good. Our ultimate and even immediate good never escapes His good purpose. Selflessness, this mark of grace, operates from the overwhelming consciousness of the Lord's presence: "The Lord is at hand." No matter what life brings, no one ever loses who lives in the reality of the presence of Christ. "The Lord is nigh unto all them that call upon him" (Psalm 145:18).

Third, relax (4:6-7). Too many of us have a nervous faith. It is one thing to believe, another to relax in the certainty of what we believe and know to be true. It is so easy for our minds to stampede out of control and kick up the dust of doubt that obscures the truth from our sight. Paul tells us nervous believers to be careful for nothing. Anxiety destroys the peace of mind that is Christ's legacy to us (John 14:27). If relaxing is hindered by worry, it is attained through prayer. We have already learned from Daniel that prayer is an essential means of grace that God has given to us to accomplish His will. Prayer is the means whereby our wills conform to His. As we entrust ourselves and our cares to the Lord and His control, He causes His peace to stand guard around our hearts, calming the fears and giving assurance that all is well. Significantly, this mission of peace flows through Jesus Christ, and leads to the final step.

Fourth, reflect on good thoughts (4:8). Christian living does not occur in a mental vacuum. Since behavior flows from thinking, it is imperative that we think correctly. I don't know exactly how the brain works, but it seems to be a law that persistent thoughts create grooves in the brain that are difficult to eradicate. That is true for good or bad thoughts: Think about something long enough and it's hard not to think about it. Paul provides a list of thoughts that ought to groove the Christian's brain: "whatsoever things are true, whatsoever things are honest, whatsoever things are just, whatsoever things are pure, whatsoever things are lovely, whatsoever things are of good report; if there be any virtue, and if there be any praise, think on these things." Suffice it to say that all these signify perfections of Christ Himself and point to Him. Consequently, we can sum up Paul's list with the admonition to think about Christ. Grooving the mind with thoughts of Christ eliminates the possibility of anxiety, fear, or doubt. God promises perfect peace for those whose minds and thoughts are propped up by Him and by the truth of His word: "Thou wilt keep him in perfect peace, whose mind is stayed on thee" (Isaiah 26:3). In many ways, the preceding three steps to peace and contentment in time depend on the execution of step four. Christ is the answer to everything; He is the key to understanding time.

We learned from Daniel that Christ is the center and climax of all history. It makes sense, then, that if we are going to understand our place in time, we must do so in terms of Jesus Christ. Every proper view of time looks ahead to eternity. It is of eternal importance that first and foremost we know Christ personally as our Savior. Without Christ, time in this world is the best it will ever be regardless of how bad the times. An eternity of damnation is the destiny of every soul outside of the Lord Jesus Christ. With Christ, time in this world is the worst it will ever be regardless of how good the times. Believers leave this world to be with Christ, which is far better. It is of temporal importance that we who know the Lord Jesus rely on the revealed truth that nothing in life can really be against us (Romans 8:31). Faith lays hold of what it knows: "We know that all things work together for good to them that love God, to them who are the called according to his purpose" (Romans 8:28). This is the bottom line, and it is a good place to stop and to rest. Daniel has supplied ample evidence of its truth. May the Holy Spirit graciously convince us of its truth personally. If this study of God's sure providence and unfailing purpose has helped to further a biblical understanding of time and has impressed on us the importance of living in Christ, I give my humble thanks to the Lord. ⚜

APPENDIX I

CHARTS

THE TIMES OF DANIEL (+ OR -)

JUDAH	BABYLON	MEDIA-PERSIA
		Astyages, king of Media (585-550)
	Neo-Babylonian Empire established (626)	Cyrus' conquest of Media-beginning of Persian Empire (550)
Josiah (640-609) killed at Megiddo by Necho II	Nabopolassar (626-605)	
Jehoahaz (609) captured by Egyptians	Alliance with Medes to destroy Ninevah (612)	
Jehoiakim (609-598) Daniel's exile (605)	Battle of Carchemish (605)	Cyrus (550-530)
Jehoiachin (597-587) deportation to Babylon (597)	Nebuchadnezzar (605-562)	Cambyses (530-522)
Zedekiah (597-587) Fall of Jerusalem & deportation to Babylon (587/586)	Amel-Marduk (562-560)	Darius I (522-486)
	Neriglissar (560-556)	Xerxes (486-465)
Babylonian Exile (587-538)	Labashi-Marduk (556)	Artaxerxes I (465-424)
Edict of Cyrus to return (538)	Nabonidus (556-539)	Darius II (423-404)
Sheshbazzar's return (538)	Belshazzar as co-regent	
Zerubbabel's return (536)		
Temple finished (516)	Fall of Babylon to Persia (539)	
Time of Esther (479-473)		
Ezra's return (458)		
Nehemiah (445-433)		

DANIEL'S SURVEY OF HUMAN WORLD GOVERNMENT

DANIEL 2	DANIEL 7	DANIEL 8	DANIEL 11
1. Head of Gold: **Babylon**	1. Lion: **Babylon**		
2. Breast & arms of silver: **Medo-Persia**	2. Bear: **Medo-Persia**	2. Ram: **Medo-Persia**	
3. Belly & thighs of bronze: **Greece**	3. Leopard: **Greece**	3. Male Goat: **Greece** a. Large horn: **Alexander** b. 4 horns: **his successors**	3. Kingdom of Greece a. Mighty king: **Alexander** b. Division of kingdom into 4 c. The base king: **Antiochus**
4. Legs of iron & feet of iron/clay: **Rome & its continuation**	4. Dreadful beast: **Rome (10 horns: 10 kings)**		
5. The Stone: **God's Kingdom**	5. Receiving the Kingdom by the Son of Man		
	6. The little horn: **AntiChrist** a. Remarkable eyes b. Boastful mouth c. Power over saints d. Changes times & laws e. Absolute rule for 3½ times f. Dominion destroyed	6. The little horn: **Antiochus Epiphanes** **(a type of AntiChrist)**	6. The willful king: a. Speaks against God b. Spurns all gods except power c. Fights kings of north & south d. Finally destroyed

MAPS OF THE FINAL FOUR + ONE

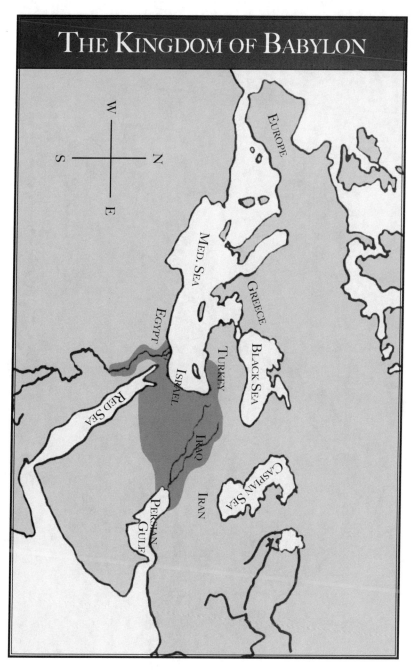

THE KINGDOM OF BABYLON

NOTE: THE SHADED AREAS MARK THE BORDERS OF THE KINGDOM.

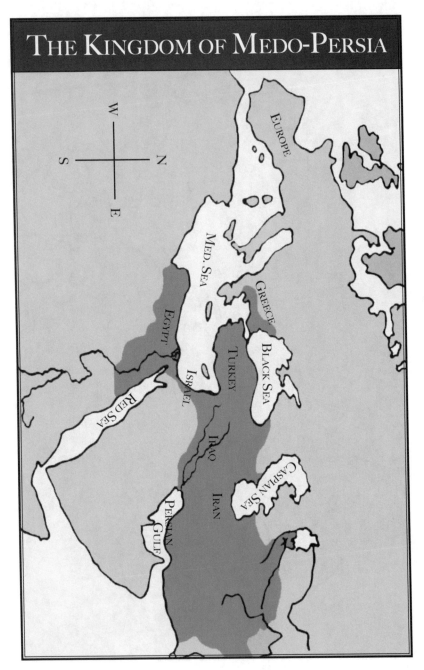

THE KINGDOM OF MEDO-PERSIA

NOTE: THE SHADED AREAS MARK THE BORDERS OF THE KINGDOM.

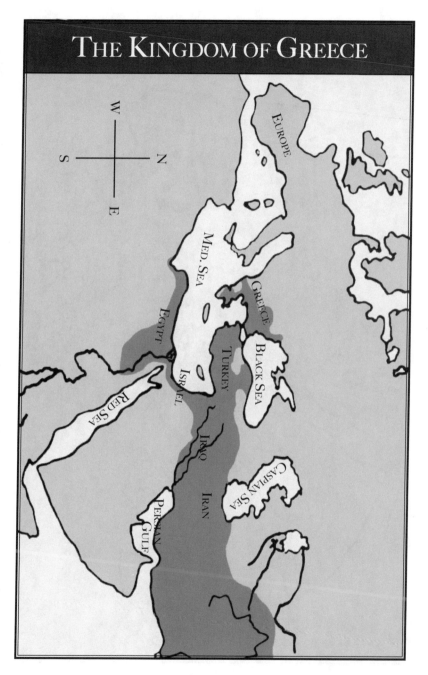

NOTE: THE SHADED AREAS MARK THE BORDERS OF THE KINGDOM.

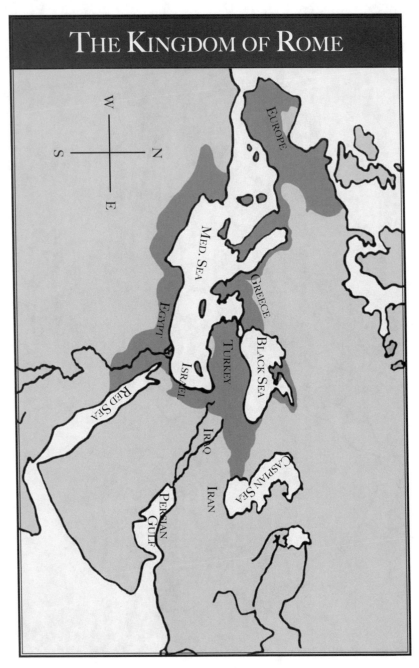

THE KINGDOM OF ROME

NOTE: THE SHADED AREAS MARK THE BORDERS OF THE KINGDOM.

THE KINGDOM OF CHRIST

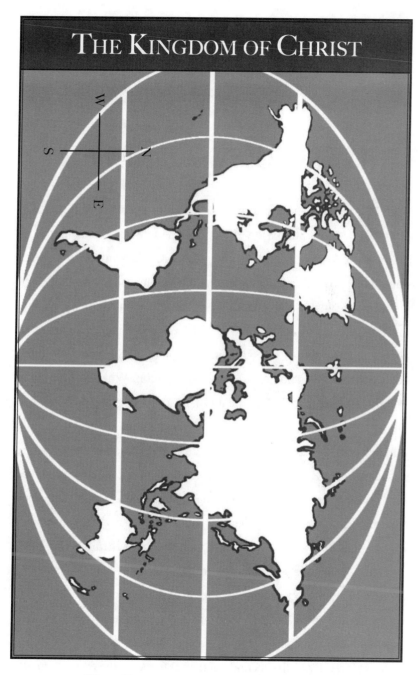

NOTE: THERE ARE NO SHADED AREAS BECAUSE
CHRIST'S KINGDOM HAS NO BORDERS.

BEFORE AND AFTER

B ased on both internal and external evidence, the standard conservative view of the Old Testament canon marks its completion no later than 424 B.C. Liberal critics, on the other hand, postpone the completion date as long as they possibly can, crediting the hypothetical Council of Jamnia with officially closing the Old Testament canon in A.D. 90. A fundamental disagreement concerning the divine origin and inspiration of all Scripture lies at the heart of this considerable difference of opinion. Whereas orthodoxy requires a belief that God, as the ultimate author of Scripture, breathed out every one of the words using human instruments to write them down, liberal critics deny the supernatural inspiration of the Scripture and claim the Bible to be nothing more than a humanly produced book with a particular religious bias and agenda. Since they deny supernatural inspiration generally, they must deny the possibility of supernatural before-the-event prophecies specifically. The Book of Daniel is a casebook example of such critical denial. Daniel 11 especially stands out because of the undeniable accuracy with which it records the events of Seleucid history. Critics are forced by their creed to date this chapter specifically as well as the apocalyptic visions generally to the second century B.C., after the events actually transpired, whereas conservatives date the composition of Daniel no later than about 530 B.C. For the liberal critic, Daniel is an after-the-event prophecy written anonymously and attributed to the sixth-century Daniel to infuse it with authority and credibility.

Something that critics deny so vehemently must really be important. For conservative believers, Daniel 11 is a remarkable before-the-event prophecy whose minute accuracy gives credence to our proposition that God governs all of time. As I emphasized in Chapter 6, notwithstanding all the intrigue, treachery, and opposition to God's plan that marked this period of history, God used the Seleucids to put in place much of what was essential for the spread of Christianity. To me, one of the great ironies is that Antioch, the city whose name commemorates a line of rulers bent on infusing Greek ideology throughout society, became the headquarters of gospel missions that commissioned the apostle Paul to evangelize the world. God always overrules evil for good as He brings to time His eternal plan.

To illustrate this remarkable predictive precision in Daniel 11, I am going to print the relevant texts from Scripture and then offer a *brief* synopsis of the fulfilled history. I simply want to plug in a few names and places without detailing every single thing that the historical records supply for our information. For those who would like to get all the details, there are plenty of ready sources. Any standard Bible encyclopedia will include relevant entries. For instance, just looking under the entries for Seleucus, Antiochus, or Ptolemy, will provide much of interest. Many commentaries on Daniel will also relate the events of history to the text in Daniel. Gleason Archer's contribution in volume 7 of *The Expositor's Bible Commentary* series is a good example. Any book that deals with the history of Israel will have a section dealing with the Intertestamental period. These are all secondary sources but helpful. If someone prefers a detailed account of this period from the Jewish perspective, he can check out 1 and 2 Maccabees. I know these are apocryphal books and consequently without inspired authority, but let's not dismiss them summarily for that reason. They suffer from the same set of limitations as any secular history (i.e., the imperfect knowledge and bias of the author), but they are, nonetheless, credible and useful. Virtually every modern review of this era that I have ever read relies significantly on the Maccabean accounts. Written originally in Hebrew sometime between 163 and 135 B.C., 1 Maccabees is close enough to the events recorded that most scholars agree to its overall historical accuracy. Second Maccabees, written in Greek about 40 B.C., is more theologically biased than 1 Maccabees but still an important witness. Josephus also reviews this crucial period in *The Antiquities of the Jews*, Book 12. I wouldn't be surprised, however, if he used the books of Maccabees as a reference himself. The Greek historian Polybius (200-120 B.C.) contributes some information to our corpus of knowledge, but his *Histories* is incomplete and what remains is more difficult to access. The point is that if someone wants more information than I am going to give, there are plenty of places to find it.

As we compare Daniel's prophecy with what we know from history, I want us to see it as a story told before and after. It is remarkable evidence not only of God's knowledge of time but also of His use of it to accomplish His purpose. Before reviewing the story, let me give the cast of characters.

THE CAST OF CHARACTERS

Alexander the Great
(336-323 B.C.)

THE LINE OF PTOLEMY	THE LINE OF SELEUCUS
Ptolemy I (Soter) (323-285 B.C.)	Seleucus I (Nicator) (312-281 B.C.)
Ptolemy II (Philadelphus) (285-246 B.C.)	Antiochus I (Soter) (281-261 B.C.)
Ptolemy III (Euergetes) (246-221 B.C.)	Antiochus II (Theos) (261-246 B.C.)
	Seleucus II (Callinicus) (246-226 B.C.)
	Seleucus III (Ceraunus) (226-223 B.C.)
Ptolemy IV (Philopater) (221-203 B.C.)	Antiochus III (Great) (223-187 B.C.)
Ptolemy V (Epiphanes) (203-181 B.C.)	Seleucus IV (Philophater) (187-175 B.C.)
Ptolemy VI (Philometer) (281-146 B.C.)	Antiochus IV (Epiphanes) (175-164/163 B.C.)

THE BEFORE AND AFTER STORY

BEFORE

11:1-5 Also I in the first year of Darius the Mede, even I, stood to confirm and to strengthen him. And now will I shew thee the truth. Behold, there shall stand up yet three kings in Persia; and the fourth shall be far richer than they all: and by his strength through his riches he shall stir up all against the realm of Grecia. And a mighty king shall stand up, that shall rule with great dominion, and do according to his will. And when he shall stand up, his kingdom shall be broken, and shall be divided toward the four winds of heaven; and not to his posterity, nor according to his dominion which he ruled: for his kingdom shall be plucked up, even for others beside those. And the king of the south shall be strong, and one of his princes; and he shall be strong above him, and have dominion; his dominion shall be a great dominion.

AFTER

Sometime after the death of Alexander, his empire was divided among his generals because his sons were incompetent. Initially, Seleucus I (Nicator) was subordinate to Ptolemy I (Soter) of Egypt– "one of his princes." Eventually, Seleucus gained control of Syria and took the title of king for himself. Ptolemy assumed the same title over Egypt. A rivalry soon developed between the two kingdoms with the balance of power shifting often. Since Palestine was the land bridge between Syria and Egypt, it was frequently caught in the middle of the conflicts between the two rivals.

BEFORE

11:6 And in the end of years they shall join themselves together; for the king's daughter of the south shall come to the king of the north to make an agreement: but she shall not retain the power of the arm; neither shall he stand, nor his arm: but she shall be given up, and they that brought her, and he that begat her, and he that strengthened her in these times.

AFTER

Ptolemy II (Philadelphus) gave his daughter Berenice in marriage to Antiochus II (Theos) in order to arrange some peace accord. The precondition for this alliance required Antiochus to divorce Laodice, the wife he already had. Laodice felt betrayed, set up a rival "queendom," and waited for the opportunity to get even. Eventually, in her anger over the whole affair, she murdered both Berenice and Berenice's infant son that she had by Antiochus, insuring that her own son Seleucus II would inherent the throne. Strangely enough, Antiochus himself was poisoned. So much for peace.

BEFORE

11:7-9 But out of a branch of her roots shall one stand up in his estate, which shall come with an army, and shall enter into the fortress of the king of the north, and shall deal against them, and shall prevail: And shall also carry captives into Egypt their gods, with their princes, and with their precious vessels of silver and of gold; and he shall continue more years than the king of the north. So the king of the south shall come into his kingdom, and shall return into his own land.

After

Ptolemy III (Euergetes), the brother of Berenice, retaliated against the Seleucids in vengeance for his sister's death. He captured Antioch, a Seleucid fortress, exiling some of the nobility and looting the fortress of over 40,000 talents of silver and 2,500 vessels of gold. Upon returning to Egypt, the high priest dubbed him with the name "Euergetes," meaning Benefactor, because he brought back to Egypt some of the treasures looted by the Persians centuries earlier.

Before

11:10 But his sons shall be stirred up, and shall assemble a multitude of great forces: and one shall certainly come, and overflow, and pass through: then shall he return, and be stirred up, even to his fortress.

After

Two of the sons of Seleucus II, whose territory was invaded by Ptolemy III, sought revenge in turn. Seleucus III made the first move, but his incompetence as a military commander caused his own generals to poison him. Antiochus III, on the other hand, enjoyed limited success where his brother had failed. He marched relentlessly toward the south, seizing Ptolemaic territory in Phoenicia and gaining some control over Palestine.

Before

11:11-13 And the king of the south shall be moved with choler, and shall come forth and fight with him, even with the king of the north: and he shall set forth a great multitude; but the multitude shall be given into his hand. And when he hath taken away the multitude, his heart shall be lifted up; and he shall cast down many ten thousands: but he shall not be strengthened by it. For the king of the north shall return, and shall set forth a multitude greater than the former, and shall certainly come after certain years with a great army and with much riches.

AFTER

It was the south's turn to retaliate; the triumph of Antiochus was short-lived. The southern king, now Ptolemy IV, ousted Antiochus III at Raphia in Gaza on the southern border of Palestine. He forced the Seleucid occupation to retreat from Palestine, and for a while both Phoenicia and Palestine returned to Ptolemaic control. Thirteen years later (204/203 B.C.), Antiochus III again moved against Egypt, an act prompted specifically by the death of Ptolemy IV.

BEFORE

11:14-17 And in those times there shall many stand up against the king of the south: also the robbers of thy people shall exalt themselves to establish the vision; but they shall fall. So the king of the north shall come, and cast up a mount, and take the most fenced cities: and the arms of the south shall not withstand, neither his chosen people, neither shall there be any strength to withstand. But he that cometh against him shall do according to his own will, and none shall stand before him: and he shall stand in the glorious land, which by his hand shall be consumed. He shall also set his face to enter with the strength of his whole kingdom, and upright ones with him; thus shall he do: and he shall give him the daughter of women, corrupting her: but she shall not stand on his side, neither be for him.

AFTER

Antiochus III was able to secure Palestine and, with the help of some Jewish revolutionaries, was able to take control of Sidon.

Unexpectedly, his plans to invade Egypt itself were thwarted by Egypt's appeal to Rome for support. Antiochus was forced to play politics and temporarily set aside his military agenda. He proposed a peace agreement with Egypt by promising his daughter Cleopatra to Ptolemy V in marriage. Espionage rather than peace, however, was his intent. He had hoped his daughter would pass on Egypt's military secrets to him, but his plan backfired when Cleopatra remained loyal to her husband. Romance ruled.

BEFORE

11:18-19 After this shall he turn his face unto the isles, and shall take many: but a prince for his own behalf shall cause the reproach offered by him to cease; without his own reproach he shall cause it to turn upon him. Then he shall turn his face toward the fort of his own land: but he shall stumble and fall, and not be found.

AFTER

Antiochus III had entered an alliance with the Carthaginian general Hannibal and turned his attention to Rome. Together they invaded Greece, but Rome thwarted their advance. Hannibal escaped, but the Roman Scipio Asiaticus defeated Antiochus at Magnesia (not far from Ephesus on coast of Asia Minor). The Romans demanded he refrain from further military operations, disarmed him of his navy and war elephants, forced him to pay fifteen thousand talents, and took his son Antiochus IV hostage as collateral until the debt was paid in full. In order to fund his payments to Rome, Antiochus tried to plunder the temple of Bel at Susa in the territory of Elam, part of old Persia, which was now within the borders of Seleucia. He failed in this attempt and was killed.

BEFORE

11:20 Then shall stand up in his estate a raiser of taxes in the glory of the kingdom: but within few days he shall be destroyed, neither in anger, nor in battle.

AFTER

Seleucus IV, the next king of Syria, inherited the debt to Rome from his father and had no recourse but to pay the debt with increased taxes throughout the realm. Although he operated a policy of toleration toward the subjects of his kingdom, and Jerusalem itself had benefited from that policy, the enormous debt forced him to change course and ultimately even to plunder the temple in Jerusalem in his desperation for funds. For some reason, he exchanged his own son Demetrius for his brother Antiochus IV who had been hostage in Rome. The wisdom of this hostage exchange was questionable; mysteriously, Seleucus IV was murdered.

BEFORE

11:21 And in his estate shall stand up a vile person, to whom they shall not give the honour of the kingdom: but he shall come in peaceably, and obtain the kingdom by flatteries.

AFTER

Thanks to his father's diplomatic exchange, Demetrius, the legitimate heir to the throne, was hostage in Rome. Another son of Seleucus IV was too young to rule. Antiochus IV, the brother of Seleucus IV, had been released from banishment in Rome in exchange for Demetrius, and he aspired to the throne. Although he was not the people's choice, shrewd politicking and perhaps fratricide gained him the throne.

BEFORE

11:22-24 And with the arms of a flood shall they be overflown from before him, and shall be broken; yea, also the prince of the covenant. And after the league made with him he shall work deceitfully: for he shall come up, and shall become strong with a small people. He shall enter peaceably even upon the fattest places of the province; and he shall do that which his fathers have not done, nor his fathers' fathers; he shall scatter among them the prey, and spoil, and riches: yea, and he shall forecast his devices against the strong holds, even for a time.

AFTER

With a relatively small army, Antiochus IV rose to power and enjoyed significant victories, always with an eye toward Egypt. Like his predecessors, he employed one of the chief means of unifying the Seleucid kingdom by implementing Hellenic culture as much as possible. Unlike his predecessors, he also gained loyalty among his subjects by sharing the spoils of his conquests. His reign was marked by both generosity and tyranny. His seeming instability caused some (most likely behind his back) to nickname him "Epimanes" (crazy), a play on his own chosen nickname "Epiphanes" (manifest).

BEFORE

11:25-27 And he shall stir up his power and his courage against the king of the south with a great army; and the king of the south shall be stirred up to battle with a very great and mighty army; but he shall not stand: for they shall forecast devices against him. Yea, they that feed of the portion of his meat shall destroy him, and his army shall overflow: and many shall fall down slain. And both these kings' hearts shall be to do mischief, and they shall speak lies at one table; but it shall not prosper: for yet the end shall be at the time appointed.

AFTER

Antiochus IV achieved some initial success against Egypt with a victory over Ptolemy VI, who was betrayed by his own men. Using politics and diplomacy to his advantage, he made and broke treaties with Egypt in an effort to pit Ptolemy VI and Ptolemy VII, rivals to the throne, against each other.

BEFORE

11:28 Then shall he return into his land with great riches; and his heart shall be against the holy covenant; and he shall do exploits, and return to his own land.

AFTER

On his way home from Egypt, Antiochus learned of a rumor circulating in Palestine that he had been killed in Egypt. This rumor enraged him, and he vented his wrath against Israel by attacking Jerusalem, plundering the temple, killing forty thousand Jews, and enslaving many others. If not crazy, he acted as though he were.

BEFORE

11:29-35 At the time appointed he shall return, and come toward the south; but it shall not be as the former, or as the latter. For the ships of Chittim shall come against him: therefore he shall be grieved, and return, and have indignation against the holy covenant: so shall he do; he shall even return, and have intelligence with them that forsake the holy covenant. And arms shall stand on his part, and they shall pollute the sanctuary of strength, and shall take away the daily sacrifice, and they shall place the abomination that maketh desolate. And such as do wickedly against the covenant shall he corrupt by flatteries: but the people that do know their God shall be strong, and do exploits. And they that understand among the people shall instruct many: yet they shall fall by the sword, and by flame, by captivity, and by spoil, many days. Now when they shall fall, they shall be holpen with a little help: but many shall cleave to them with flatteries. And some of them of understanding shall fall, to try them, and to purge, and to make them white, even to the time of the end: because it is yet for a time appointed.

AFTER

In 168 B.C., Antiochus IV returned to Egypt, but this time circumstances were different. Egypt was united, and it had enlisted help from Rome. The Romans (ships of Chittim) sent Popilius Laenas to intercept Antiochus and to warn him not to attack Egypt unless he wanted to fight against Rome as well. According to the well-known and oft-repeated story, the Roman drew a circle around Antiochus and demanded his response before he stepped out of the circle. Antiochus meekly submitted and acquiesced to the demands. But he became furious and on his retreat took out his rage on Palestine. This is the event that precipitated the most heinous acts against Israel. He desecrated the temple and set up shrines to Greek gods throughout the land. He imposed restrictions on many of the Jewish customs, threatening death for noncompliance. These atrocities incited the Maccabean revolt in which many valiant Jews died for their faith, and sadly many others betrayed their own countrymen.

The "before" story continues by jumping ahead to the final Antichrist. As of now, there is no after story. But it will come. ✧

APPENDIX 4

THEOLOGY FOR LIFE *

By MICHAEL P. V. BARRETT

There is hardly another book of the Bible more maligned, misunderstood, and ignored than the book of Ecclesiastes. Without question the book has many surface problems that must be resolved and explained in the light of the specific contexts and overall message and intent of the book. The easy solution of declaring the book to be nothing more than the product of man's reasoning should be rejected in view of the book's divine inspiration and consequent profitability for doctrine, reproof, correction, and instruction in righteousness. The message of Ecclesiastes had its origin in the One Great Shepherd, the Lord God Himself, who graciously revealed His upright and true words (12:10, 11) to the Preacher (Qoheleth) for man's good. This book declares the philosophy of life, the world view, that ought to govern the life of every believer and attract every sinner to the Lord. Unless man, whether saint or sinner, understands and implements this message, the real meaning and purpose of life will remain a mystery with frustration and despair ruling. To seek satisfaction and contentment in the things of life is to look in the wrong place. The message of Ecclesiastes constantly points to the

* Reprinted with permission from Biblical Viewpoint, XXXI (November, 1997), 11-18

Eternal God who only can satisfy man and requires that the "stuff" of time be evaluated and used in light of the certain reality of eternity. How we view the Lord determines how we view life. How we view life is a mirror of how we view the Lord. Recognizing and submitting to the Lord God is essential to a Biblical philosophy of life. Qoheleth draws attention to four key truths about God and their implications in establishing a theology for life.

GOD IS THE POWERFUL CREATOR

Throughout Scripture God's creating work testifies to His infinite power, wisdom, and glory. Only God has the power and ability to create, and all that He has created in one way or another testifies to and reveals His awesome glory. There is hardly a more foundational theological truth than the fact that God is the Creator. The inescapable implication of this basic truth is that God, therefore, owns everything, including us. To admit that we belong to the Lord by virtue of His creating us will impact our understanding and experience of life. Qoheleth's orthodox declaration of God the Creator is threefold.

First, He *made everything*. In 11:5 Qoheleth describes God as the one who made all. In 3:11, the theme verse of the book, he explicitly declares that God has made everything beautiful. The language is all inclusive; God made the "totality." Whatever exists God has made, by Himself, for Himself, for His pleasure and glory (cf. Col. 1:16, 17). The vastness, complexities, and details of the creation are ultimately incomprehensible to man, and that itself ought to draw man to that One who in infinitely superior. Everything in this world belongs to the Creator, and there is no possibility of ultimately understanding anything apart from God. To believe that this world is the result of some chance and random evolution of chaos to order is to wander blindly and aimlessly, stumbling to nowhere. There should be little wonder that so many in this world are in constant despair as they vainly search for the meaning of life while denying that God is the Creator. On the other hand, to believe that this world is the work of an all wise, powerful Creator gives the foundation of reason and logic to all that is, even when the reason for things remains hidden to us. Faith knows there is reason because there is a Creator.

Second, *He made man.* The Genesis account of the original creation reveals that although man shares much in common with other created life forms, he is unique in that he is in the image of God; man marks the climax, the apex of God's creating work. Man is a spiritual, ultimately immortal being with intellect, emotion, and will, created in original righteousness, holiness, and knowledge, with dominion over the rest of creation. A proper philosophy of life must recognize that man is personally accountable to the Creator and that man's unique place in this world is due not to the struggling of the species to survive, but to the design of God.

Qoheleth echoes Genesis. After lamenting the deplorable state of humanity in general (7:25–28), Qoheleth acknowledges that "God hath made man upright" (7:29). The word "upright" refers to man's ethical, not physical posture. It speaks of man's original state of innocence, including that straight and righteous status before the Lord. Qoheleth seems to understand by this word the pre-fall nature of that divine image: righteousness, true holiness, knowledge (cf. Eph. 4:24; Col. 3:10). The Preacher also acknowledges the uniqueness of man from the rest of creation when declaring that God set "eternity" in man's heart (3:11). There is something about man that will live forever and cannot, therefore, be satisfied with temporal things. The tragedy is that in spite of what God made man, man by his sin rejected the knowledge of God, lost his righteousness, and gives himself to the pursuit of his own schemes and plans (7:29b). It is part of sin to ignore the Creator. Qoheleth's investigation of life and experience revealed that the more man follows his own imagination in trying to find meaning, purpose, and satisfaction in life, the further he removes himself from the Lord, and the more desperate life becomes. That man denies his accountability and responsibility to the Creator does not abrogate that duty; it only jeopardizes his immortal soul. What the Preacher observed in his generation is certainly true in ours; there is nothing new under the sun.

Third, *He made me.* The doctrine of creation, like all doctrine, must be personalized if it is to have practical influence in daily living. In his closing argument, Qoheleth issued the imperative, "remember now **thy** Creator" (12:1). Remembering is an act of the will. It means to consciously bring something to mind, to make oneself think about something on purpose. A Christian philosophy of life requires that every believer bring to bear on the issues of life the fact that God made him. The implications of this personalized truth are far-reaching. We must be satisfied that God has made us as so pleased Him. Our existence is not an accident, nor just a biological phenomenon. We are, each one, "fearfully and wonderfully made" (Ps. 139:14). When God made us according to His pleasure, He did a good job. We should not question or fret over how He made us. We are accountable to God for what He has made us, not for what He has not made us. Too many Christians tend to compare themselves with others and wish they were different. Because they are not different, they feel sorry for themselves.

Whether we are short or tall, black or white, smart or dumb, athletic or clumsy, musical or not, we are what He made us to be. What lesser of God's creation ever complains or feels sorry for itself because it is not something else? If every other facet of creation constantly declares God's glory (Ps. 19), how much more should we.

GOD IS THE WISE SOVEREIGN

The next life affecting truth is that God is the all wise Sovereign and therefore, He preserves and rules us. Providence is the constant and ordinary work of God whereby He preserves and governs His creation to the designed end of His glory. Included in that glory is the ultimate good of God's people. Belief in the sovereign providence of God is the very opposite of fatalism. The affairs of life do not happen by blind chance; they happen as they are orchestrated in perfect harmony by an all wise God who both knows and determines the end from the beginning. Qoheleth declares that "the righteous, and the wise, and their works, are in the hand of God" (9:1). Not only are the affairs of life in God's hand, His purposes are secure and unfrustratable: "I know that, whatsoever God doeth, it shall be for ever: nothing can be put to it, nor any thing taken from it: and God doeth it, that men should fear before him" (3:14). Living in the constant awareness of God (i.e., fearing Him) puts a spiritual slant on things that is essential to a Biblical philosophy of life. Providence assures us that there is a reason for everything, even though that reason may be hidden from our understanding. Faith lays hold of God and dispels the despair that so frequently grips us when we consider life apart from God. Three summary statements personalize Ecclesiastes' teaching concerning this important truth.

First, *God determines my times*. Believing that God determines our times means that there is no better time for us to live than now. Qoheleth warns against the folly of longing for the "good ole days" (7:10); there is no such thing. Learn the lessons from the past; prepare for the future; but live now. The best way to live now is by faith in the all wise Sovereign. Ecclesiastes 3:1–8, 11 is a vital text. There is a time and purpose for everything that happens. In verses 1-8 Qoheleth employs literary genius to substantiate his conclusion in verse 11 that God has made everything appropriate in this time. A series of fourteen pairs of twenty-eight specific times that have been purposed give the overall impression that in the will of God there is a time for absolutely everything. All the occasions of life are part of the divine order. The twenty-eight specific times mentioned are a sort of *brachylogy* (a condensed expression to designate the totality of an idea) and include, therefore, all kinds of time. The fourteen pairs are expressed as *merismus* (the linking of opposite terms to designate totality). For example, a time to be born and a time to die identify not only the moments of birth and death, but encompass all the moments in between.

Although the language intends to convey the idea of inclusiveness, the particular times mentioned are instructive. Throughout this list of times are important lessons. A practical belief in the Sovereignty of God (that He determines the times of life) will enable us to live through the vicissitudes of life with confidence and good sense. Good sense always accompanies good theology. For instance, weeping and mourning are among the times of life ordained as appropriate (3:4). Trusting the sovereignty of God does not demand a stoic response to tragedy. Stoicism is not faith. Faith weeps in weeping times while resting contentedly in the Lord's always good will. Not sorrowing as the world sorrows does not mean not sorrowing at all. We must learn to trust and pray that God will enable us to use and experience all our times to His glory.

Second, *He determines my circumstances.* One of the common themes in Ecclesiastes is that God has given us our lot or portion in life. A proper philosophy of life requires contentment and satisfaction with what He has given us. Discontentment usually comes when we pout over what we do not have in comparison with someone else. Over and again Qoheleth identifies the many gifts God has given His people for their good. For example, He has given us our families. In 9:9 he issues the imperative to "live joyfully with the wife whom thou lovest . . . which he hath given thee . . . for that is thy portion in this life . . . ." What the Authorized Version translates "live joyfully" literally is "see life." To see life is to experience life. God has made man to be a social being, and the bedrock of society and social relationships is the family, the foundation of which is the union between husband and wife. By logical extension this includes not just the marriage relationship, but the whole family structure as one of the great treasures of life from the Lord. It does not take much experience in living to realize how important the family is to the whole welfare of society. If we do not delight in the families God has given us, there is little chance that we can know contentment in any thing else. A good home with a good relationship between husband and wife can erase a lot of the mundane cares of life. Enjoying the family that the Lord has ordained is a key element in a God-centered philosophy of life. Qoheleth's theology here parallels Moses' who compares a family life that operates with constant reference to the Lord to "days of heaven upon the earth" (Deut. 11:21).

Another key example of divinely determined circumstance concerns our vocations. This along with family probably encompasses more of daily life than anything else. God has given us our labor and the ability to enjoy it (2:10, 24; 3:13; 5:18); therefore, we should work diligently to His glory (9:10). It is tragic that so many people, even Christians, hate what they have to do to make a living. Granted, there is a curse associated with labor, but labor itself is not the curse. Not only is labor a practical means of providing for the essentials of life, it is a means of occupying the times of life. Idleness serves no good purpose. The profit of labor is not in what is left over, but in taking full advantage of the experience. The profitability of labor is not to be judged by what pays the most or makes the most contribution to humanity; all that is vanity and will soon fade as vapor. To acknowledge that even the most ordinary work is God's providential gift will encourage faithful and diligent operation of that labor to the glory of God. For a Christian there is no labor more important than what God has given. Whether in the pulpit, or in the factory, or in the home, God-given labor ought to be source of contentment and pleasure in this temporary world.

Third, *He determines everything for my good.* This is the bottom line. A Christian philosophy of life trusts the Lord that He knows and does what is best for His people. That the Lord regards His people as special and treats them differently than sinners is a glorious truth of the Gospel. Qoheleth believed, like Paul, that all things work together for good to those who love God. According to Qoheleth, whereas God gives the sinner travail, He gives the man who is good before Him wisdom, knowledge, and joy (2:26): the skill to live and the capacity to be content. But whatever the particular manifestations of God's governing our times and circumstances (whether "good" times or "bad"). His purpose is to bring us to greater faith and dependence on

Him. Ecclesiastes 7:14 says it all. God juxtaposes the good days and bad days for the purpose of bringing us to the end of ourselves and finding complete satisfaction in the Lord Himself. Whenever God's people come to depend on Him completely, that is their good. It is good and comforting to know that "the righteous, and wise, and their works, are in the hand of God" (9:1).

GOD IS THE INFALLIBLE JUDGE

Throughout the experience of God's people in every generation, the anomalies of justice and apparent inequities of life have been a test to faith and potential hindrance to a proper view of life itself. It was part of Qoheleth's observation of life that wickedness was in the place of judgment and iniquity was in the place of righteousness (3:16). That God is the infallible Judge of every man assures that justice will prevail. Indeed, the doctrine of the final judgment ought to be a deterrent to sin as well as a source of consolation for the godly in times of adversity because it guarantees that all will be well in the end.

Qoheleth emphasizes two essential truths concerning God's judgment. First, *His judgment is absolutely comprehensive.* The final word of the book is that "God shall bring every work into judgment, with every secret thing, whether it be good, or whether it be evil" (12:14). Based on infinite knowledge, God's judgment will make no mistakes and therefore, no excuses will provide defense in that day. To know that He knows ought to stop us short of sin, guard us in temptations, and guide us to holiness. To live in the reality that "all things are naked and opened unto the eyes of him with whom we have to do" (Heb. 4:13) ought throughout the course of our lives be an incentive to purity.

Second, *His judgment is certain.* Qoheleth's theology equals the New Testament: "it is appointed unto men once to die, but after this the judgment" (Heb. 9:27). A main thrust of Qoheleth's teaching is to live with the "after this" in mind. In 11:9, 10 he encourages the young man to rejoice and take full advantage of life, but with a view to the certainty that "for all these things God will bring thee into judgment." He then makes the appropriate application to remove irritation from the heart and put away evil form the flesh: in other words, to be content with the life God has given and to strive to be holy. A proper philosophy of life requires living with eternity in sight; true happiness and contentment *now* is possible only with a view to *then*. This life is not all there is; in fact, it is only a small portion of what really is. The certainty of judgment, the day of reckoning, is also a guarantee of justice and terror to the ungodly. Qoheleth warns sinners not to interpret the delay of justice to mean that justice will not come: "Though a sinner do evil a hundred times . . . it shall not be well with the wicked . . ." (8:11–13). The current anomalies of justice that are so common will be set right when "God shall judge the righteous and the wicked" (3:17). This is part of God's unfrustratable purpose (3:17).

GOD IS THE SUPREME REALITY

Man's inability to know is a prominent theme in Ecclesiastes: whether the "why'" of life or the "what's" of the future (e.g., 6: 12; 9:1, 10, 12, 10:14; 11:2, 6). This ignorance can easily produce anxiety, feelings of uncertainty, and questions concerning the ultimate realities and meaning of life. Throughout his investigation, Qoheleth constantly draws away from the things of life as the answer to any of the ultimate questions. After all is said and done, his conclusion is that everything in life is vanity (a breath that is fleeting and unsubstantial) and that the "totality" for man is to fear God and keep His commandments (12:8, 13). Fearing God and obeying God always go together. This is the bottom line for a Christian philosophy of life. Although there are several elements and implications of fearing God, the concept can best be summarized as living in the awareness of God. The more we are aware of the Lord, the better we will live. He is the Supreme Reality; nothing is more real or absolute than He. Living in the conscious awareness that God is real is more than just jargon or creedal affirmation; it must be the mindset of every believer. The believer must consciously factor in the reality of God to every situation and circumstance of life.

Three observations are possible from Qoheleth's attention to the fear of God. First, *fearing God is the secret to trusting Him concerning all the uncertainties of life.* The things about life that defy explanation are themselves evidence of the Lord God who made things that way (3:11–14; 8:17). The fact that we cannot understand all or alter His purposes is designed to draw us to Him: "God doeth it, that men should fear before him" (3:14). Faith rests in the reality that He does all well.

Second, *fearing God is an aid to worship.* Ecclesiastes 5:1–7 establish significant guidelines for proper and spiritual worship of the Infinitely Superior Supreme Reality. Verses 7 summarizes the required self-restraint, sincere submission, and spiritual sacrifice with the imperative "fear thou God." Worship is an essential part of Christian living. Conscious awareness of how great God is will generate a worship of reverence, awe, and respect. A true and proper fear of God teaches that worship is service to Him and not entertainment for us.

Third, *fearing God is the defense for the judgment*. What happens in eternity is infinitely more important than what happens in life. Ecclesiastes 8:12 assures that "it shall be well with them that fear God, which fear before him." This fear must be understood in its full theological and evangelical significance. To fear God is to know Him as He reveals Himself. The same Preacher said "the fear of the LORD is the beginning knowledge" (Prov. 1:7) and "the fear of the LORD is the beginning of wisdom: and the knowledge of the holy is understanding" (Prov. 9:10). In the Old Testament, fearing God is the essence of spiritual religion and a vital relationship to the Lord. It is the beginning, the middle, and end of true life; it is the only thing that will do a man good in life and better in death. To see the final and full significance requires the definition of spiritual knowledge given by Jesus Christ: "This is life eternal, that they may know thee the only true God, and Jesus Christ, whom thou has sent: (John 17:3). It is impossible to know God, the Supreme Reality, without knowing Jesus Christ. It is only by knowing Christ as Savior that there will be salvation in the day of judgment. That has always been true. Therefore, this book that is so concerned with dealing with the issues of living finds its ultimate solution in forcing men to consider God and His gracious provisions for both this life and the life to come. ∝